John Symonds

Observations

upon the expediency of revising the present English version of the four gospels and

the Acts of the Apostles

John Symonds

Observations

upon the expediency of revising the present English version of the four gospels and the Acts of the Apostles

ISBN/EAN: 9783337285371

Printed in Europe, USA, Canada, Australia, Japan

Cover: Foto ©Lupo / pixelio.de

More available books at **www.hansebooks.com**

OBSERVATIONS
UPON THE
EXPEDIENCY OF REVISING
THE
PRESENT ENGLISH VERSION
OF THE
FOUR GOSPELS,
AND OF
THE ACTS OF THE APOSTLES.

By JOHN SYMONDS, LL.D.
PROFESSOR OF MODERN HISTORY IN THE UNIVERSITY OF CAMBRIDGE.

Quid sit turpius, quam id esse obscurum ipsum, quod in eum solum adhibetur usum, ne sint cætera obscura? QUINCTIL. Instit. L. IV. 5.

CAMBRIDGE,
Printed by J. ARCHDEACON Printer to the UNIVERSITY;
And sold by T. PAYNE & Son, Mews-gate, London; J. & J. MERRILL, and W. LUNN, Cambridge; and P. DECK, Bury St. Edmund's.
MDCCLXXXIX.

TO HIS GRACE

AUGUSTUS HENRY,

DUKE OF GRAFTON,

CHANCELLOR OF THE UNIVERSITY OF CAMBRIDGE.

MY LORD,

IF, after the example of the Antients, literary productions are to be addressed to the author's *best* friend, Your Grace's claim to the following papers is indisputable. By Your recommendation, unsolicited and even unasked, I have for many years had the honour of enjoying a distinguished appointment in this University: and, what infinitely increases my obligations to Your Grace, You have ever since ranked me in the number of Your particular friends.

Independent of these motives, the propriety of this address is justified by the nature of the work itself. From repeated conversations with You, I have had the

satis-

DEDICATION.

satisfaction to discover, that the subject of it hath frequently employed Your time and Your attention; and though I am sensible, that You will look upon compliments as ill-suiting the intimacy between us, yet it would have been highly improper, from a fear of offending Your delicacy, to forbear mentioning this fact, which, whilst it gratifies me, cannot fail of doing You credit.

JOHN SYMONDS.

Cambridge,
Feb. 12, 1789.

PREFACE.

PREFACE.

WHEN I first sat down to collect the scattered observations, which at various times I had made upon the Present Version of the New Testament, it was my design to offer the whole, or the greater part of them, to the Public; but soon after I had begun to range them in order, I found them to be much more numerous than I expected: and as I was persuaded, that it would ill become me, in my first attempt of this kind, to presume too much upon the indulgence of my reader, I determined to contract my plan; and to confine it to the four Gospels, and to the Acts of the Apostles. The publication of my remarks upon the Epistles will depend in a great measure upon the reception which may be given to the following sheets.

It will be easily perceived, that to consult so many Versions was a work both of time and fatigue. Some perhaps may be surprized, that I have had frequent recourse to the Vulgate, without paying the like attention to more antient Versions, contained in the London Polyglot, which are unquestionably very serviceable towards illustrating the Greek text; but I really thought, that it would be acting disingenuously to cite them, as I am not so fortunate as to understand the languages in which they were originally written; and I should not in any instance have consulted

PREFACE.

the Latin Verſions of them (which are merely tranſlations of tranſlations) if it had not been with a view of placing in its true light a very important paſſage in St. Luke's Goſpel. I have indeed made frequent uſe of two Verſions profeſſedly tranſlated from the Vulgate; namely, that of Wicklif, and that which is generally called the Verſion of Mons. But it is to be obſerved, that in Wicklif there are many variations from the Vulgate; and though the author of the Verſion of Mons profeſſes in his title-page to tranſlate from the Vulgate, he informs us in his preface, that he always departed from it, when it diſagreed with the Original; and, in fact, he ſo often abandoned the Vulgate, that Father Simon has paſſed a very ſevere cenſure upon him for this unfair way of proceeding. But my chief care has been to compare our preſent Verſion with ſeveral tranſlations in different languages; nor can this appear improper, if we reflect, that it was actually done by king James's tranſlators, for which they have been highly commended. We learn from Selden " that theſe tranſlators took an excellent way, that part of the Bible being given to him, who was excellent in ſuch a tongue — and then they met together, and one read the tranſlation, the reſt holding in their hands ſome Bible, either of the learned tongues, or French, Spaniſh, Italian, &c. If they found any fault, they ſpoke; if not, he read on [*]." Now, as almoſt all the Verſions cited in this eſſay were prior to that of king James's tranſlators, it cannot be unacceptable to the reader to examine, whether they availed themſelves of all the advantages which they were capable of deriving, both from the Engliſh and the foreign tranſlations.

Though I have enlarged much more upon the ambiguities in
our

---

[*] Vol. III. p. 2009. ed. Wilk.

PREFACE.

our Verſion, than upon any other defects, yet ſtill there are numberleſs inſtances which I have omitted mentioning on that head; and I deſire it may be underſtood, that I do not take upon me to enter into a full examination of our Verſion, but merely to point out the principal faults, in reſpect to the language; and, whatever opinion may be formed of the propriety of my plan, I cannot but flatter myſelf with the hopes, that ſome of my remarks may be judged uſeful towards ſhewing the neceſſity of a more accurate ſtudy of the Engliſh language, than is commonly practiced.

There is nothing which I have more ſcrupulouſly obſerved, than to render juſtice to thoſe writers, to whom I am beholden for any materials; for I look upon the character of a plagiary as utterly contemptible; but though I cannot charge myſelf with the leaſt wilful ſuppreſſion, yet, as my reading is confined within very narrow limits, I dare not affirm, that none of my remarks have been already made by others: ſhould any of them, however, appear to be anticipated, I ſhall rather derive ſatisfaction from the diſcovery, than be ſurprized, or uneaſy at it; ſince at the ſame time that it juſtifies my humble endeavours, it ſecures me from the imputation of ſingularity in the attempt, and ſtrongly confirms the neceſſity of it.

I am particularly obliged to a worthy, reſpectable, and ingenious friend, who not only aſſiſted me in correcting theſe papers before they were ſent to the Preſs, but likewiſe ſuggeſted to me ſome uſeful information: and I ſhould have acknowledged his kindneſs with ſtill greater ſatisfaction, if he had permitted me to mention his name.

P. S.

P. S. After most of the following pages were printed, I received an account of the death of my friend and neighbour the Reverend Mr. Harmer, whose works I had quoted in the course of my remarks; and since, from the experience of many years, I had an opportunity of knowing his true character, I trust, I shall be justified in making the following addition to my preface.

The reputation of Mr. Harmer, as a Scholar and a Divine, is, I believe, fully and universally established. If, as a writer, he may sometimes be thought inelegant in his style, and too minute in the investigation of facts, yet these defects are amply compensated by the general choice of his materials, and the clearness of method with which he digested and arranged them. Some books come into the world, set off with all the ornaments of language; and with their authors are soon forgotten: they resemble those meteors, which by their luminous appearance attract our notice; and almost in the same moment vanish from our sight. The credit of Mr. Harmer's writings rests upon a foundation strong and durable. He hath professedly treated a subject of the first importance, which had before been touched upon only incidentally; and, by shewing at large the wonderful conformity between the antient and modern customs in the East, hath not only thrown a considerable light upon numberless passages in the Bible, but hath opened new and fruitful sources of information for the use of future expositors.

But it would be doing great injustice to Mr. Harmer, to confine our attention to the fruits of his learning alone. As the whole purpose of his studies was to illustrate the Scriptures, so it was his constant endeavour to practice those duties, which are therein declared to be essential to the forming of a true Christian.

He

He was a man of unaffected piety: equally kind as a master, parent, and husband: meek and modest in his deportment: and invariably averse from every degree of intemperance and excess. Superior to all those narrow and illiberal prejudices, which we are apt to imbibe from education or habit, he was governed by a general principle of benevolence; and though he was commonly called the father of the Dissenters, yet his good offices were so far from being confined to those of his own communion, that he acknowledged and encouraged merit wheresoever he found it. *" I will apply to Harmer"* was the usual language of every injured person in his neighbourhood; and it seldom happened, that the aggressor was not soon induced by his persuasion to repair the injury which had been done; and I do not exaggerate, when I affirm, that there is not probably a single instance of an individual to be found, who, by a mild and seasonable interference, prevented more law-suits, than Mr. Harmer. When we reflect that all these virtues, which he so eminently possessed, were still heightened by the character of a *peacemaker*; a character, to which an Evangelical blessing is annexed, we cannot but look upon his death as a public loss: much less can we be surprized, that it should deeply affect all those who personally knew him and enjoyed his friendship — but by none is it more sincerely lamented, than by him, who offers this slender tribute of regard to his memory.

CONTENTS.

CHAPTER I.
General Observations. — — — Page 1

CHAPTER II.
Upon Perspicuity. — — — — 10

CHAPTER III.
Ambiguities occasioned by the Antecedents, to which the Relatives refer, not being clearly distinguished. — — 14

CHAPTER IV.
Ambiguities occasioned by equivocal Words or Phrases. — 47

CHAPTER V.
Ambiguities occasioned by an indeterminate Use of Prepositions. 59

CHAPTER VI.
Upon Passages ungrammatical. — — — 62

CHAPTER VII.
Upon mean and vulgar Expressions. — — 90

CHAPTER VIII.
Upon obsolete or harsh Expressions. — — — 98

CONTENTS.

CHAPTER IX.

Upon the Necessity of a Literal Translation. — Page 112

CHAPTER X.

First Exception to a Literal Translation, when the Language will not admit of it, so as to make the meaning of the Words sufficiently intelligible — — — — 123

CHAPTER XI.

Second Exception to a Literal Translation, when the Times of Verbs will not admit of it. — — — — 138

CHAPTER XII.

Third Exception to a Literal Translation, when Hebraisms or Græcisms are either redundant, or repugnant to the English Idioms. 147

CHAPTER XIII.

A Comparison of two Chapters in Cranmer's, and in the Geneva, and in the Bishops Bible, with the same Chapters in our Present Version. — — — — — 157

CHAPTER XIV.

Conclusion. — — — — — 177

CHAPTER I.

General Observations.

WHEN our Blessed Lord was asked by the disciples of the Baptist, whether he were the Messiah, he referred them to the miracles which he had wrought; and to those which he actually performed in their presence; and, as if he meant to furnish them with a more convincing proof of his Divine Mission, he concluded his reply with these remarkable words " *The poor have the gospel preached to them* *." Accordingly it appears, that he embraced every opportunity to instruct the lower ranks of people; and always expressed himself in clear and intelligible terms, unless for wise reasons he spake in parables. The language of Holy writ, in which the doctrines of our Saviour and his Apostles are recorded, was eminently calculated to answer the great purposes for which it was designed; for it was the common Greek, which prevailed through the East after the conquests of the Macedonians; and which being in general use was readily comprehended by all orders and degrees of men; and, notwithstanding the objections of fastidious critics, there is sufficient ground to imagine, that the Evangelists and Apostles would not have been so easily understood by the greater part of the Gentile

* See Isaiah LXI. 1.

converts, if they had written in the same polished style, which distinguished the most elegant Classical authors. To pursue the method of the Sacred writers, in adapting the language to the capacities of all readers, should be the aim of every translator. It is not enough to enable them to distinguish the true meaning; but the most effectual care should be taken to prevent the possibility of a misconstruction. This is a circumstance in which Christians of all denominations must concur, how much soever they may disagree in other points. The case, however, is different with many Versions; and particularly with our own, which is in present use; for whoever examines it with the least degree of attention, will find, that it is ambiguous and incorrect: even in matters of the highest importance.

There are some writers, who fairly acknowledge these mistakes and imperfections; but strenuously maintain, that to new-model, or to revise our Version, would be a rash and dangerous experiment; as it might unhinge the minds of weak Christians; and disturb the public quiet. These arguments, which are the result of timidity rather than of prudence, have been adopted in all ages, and in all countries; and have been the perpetual obstacles to improvement in several parts of Europe. But is error so valuable an inheritance, that it ought never to be relinquished? Can it be sanctified by the plea of a long prescription? Experience teaches us, that mistakes in religion are of all others the most pernicious: not only because they affect us in the most important concerns, but as they are the most difficult to be corrected; and it might almost be questioned, whether it would not be safer to take the Bible out of the hands of the common people, than to expose them to the danger of drawing false conclusions

clusions from erroneous translations; for it is doubtless much worse to be misled, than to be ignorant. In regard to the argument founded on the apprehensions of alarming the public, how specious soever it may appear to superficial readers, yet it cannot have any real weight with those, who examine and judge for themselves. We ought to form our opinions of future events, by the practice of past ages. This is the chief benefit to be derived from history. Now if we cast our eye upon the period when the present Version was made, we shall find, that the mass of the people were not agitated by those imaginary terrors, which are conjured up in our days: their curiosity was excited; and their impatience prompted them to break out into censures: not on account of the impropriety of the plan, but of the dilatory conduct of the Translators*; from whose pedantic and uncouth preface we may gather likewise, that the clamours raised against them by the Protestants were chiefly the effects of party-zeal, which is now in a great measure subsided in this country. But what may serve to put this matter beyond all doubt is, that the present Version appears to have made its way without the interposition of any authority whatsoever; for it is not easy to discover any traces of a proclamation, canon, or statute published on purpose to enforce the use of it †.

There are other writers, who warmly contend, that our Version is sufficiently clear and obvious in all things necessary to be believed and practiced; and that therefore to alter it in the least degree would be a daring and mischievous innovation. On this point I will freely join issue with them; and rest the merits of the

---

* See Johnson's historical account of the several English translations of the Bible.
† See an essay on the English translation of the Bible in the Bibliotheca Literaria.

case upon a single argument. Hath not the misinterpretation of *one word* driven thousands of well-meaning Christians from the Holy Communion? For the truth of this melancholy assertion, we may safely appeal to the masters of families, and to such as are concerned in parochial cures. It may possibly be said, that the prejudices of the common people may be removed by consulting commentaries upon Scripture; but are these to be found as well in the hovels of the poor and illiterate, as in the libraries of the rich and learned? In the reign of Edward VI. it was ordered, that Erasmus's paraphrase, translated into English, should be kept in every church for the use of the parishioners; but this custom, I believe, was soon discontinued; and it now would be a fruitless attempt to look for paraphrases in parish-churches. But perhaps it would be dangerous for the common people to have frequent recourse to *all* kinds of expositions of Scripture; for it is notorious, that some of them, in respect to the Eucharist, are more calculated to create, than to dispel scruples; and are likely to infuse into men's minds new terrors, by turning a plain religious act into a mystery: a notion, which has not the least foundation in Holy writ; and which has been of infinite disservice to Christianity. It may possibly be urged likewise, that the meaning of St. Paul is cleared up by the marginal rendering; but are Bibles with marginal renderings to be often met with in humble and mean cottages? Let us suppose, however, for the sake of argument, that these are generally purchased by the lower classes of people: what inference are they likely to draw from them? It is evident, that they must be reduced to the dilemma of distrusting either the text, or the margin. If in this instance they distrust the former, as unquestionably they ought to do, there is reason to apprehend,

that

that they will be inclined to suspect the fidelity of it in other passages, of which they have no cause to doubt. I have indeed often wondered, that our Translators should introduce a marginal reading in this place. Among the rules prescribed to them by James I. it was directed, " that no marginal notes should at all be affixed, but only for the explanation of the Hebrew or Greek words, which could not, without some circumlocution, so briefly and fitly be expressed in the text." No one can seriously affirm, that κρίμα fell under this predicament; and the same may be observed of numberless words, which are explained by marginal readings, in defiance of the king's prudent injunctions.

There are a few writers, who have had the courage and discernment to choose the just medium between the two extremes. They readily acknowledge, that our present Version does not give the full and adequate meaning of the Sacred text; and that it ought to be subjected to a revision. Were this opinion advanced by men of ordinary talents, and unknown in the republic of letters, it might reasonably be suspected to be ill-grounded; but since it is recommended and enforced by those, who have carried Sacred literature to an uncommon degree of perfection, and have opened new and various sources of information, we can hardly question the propriety of the plan, without offering violence to our own understandings. Bishop Lowth makes no scruple to affirm " that, in respect of the sense and the accuracy of interpretation, the improvements, of which our Version is capable, are great and numberless; and that the expediency of revising it grows every day more and more evident [*]." Bishop Newcome confesses " that many parts of it abound with invincible difficulties

---

[*] Preliminary dissertation on Isaiah, p. lxxii.

ties to the English reader; and that a sober and accurate revisal of it would essentially serve the cause of religion *," and to the same purport Dr. Blaney and Dr. White have employed every argument, which can be suggested by a sound judgement, and a well-guided zeal †.

As many invaluable materials have lately been laid open, which may be singularly useful towards improving our Version of the Old Testament, so we have many recent and great advantages in regard to the New; for, not to mention several learned and ingenious men, who have illustrated it by their *Critical conjectures and observations*, there are two writers, to whom the world is peculiarly indebted: I mean, Mr. Markland and Dr. Owen; who have joined to an exquisite sagacity a profound knowledge of the Classical, as well as of the Scriptural style; and have rectified some inveterate errors, which the accumulated labours of two centuries had not been able to amend.

It is not my design in this essay to examine any passages in the Old Testament; nor to touch upon any points of doctrine in the New: my sole aim is to consider, whether our Translators have expressed themselves with a sufficient degree of accuracy in their Version of the Gospels, and of the Acts of the Apostles. But before we descend to particulars, it will be proper to inquire into the grounds of an opinion, which passes among some persons for an undoubted truth; namely, that the Vulgar translation of the

---

* Preface to observations on our Blessed Lord's conduct, p. ii.—and likewise the preface to the attempt towards an improved Version of the twelve minor Prophets, p. xi.

† Preliminary discourse to the new translation of Jeremiah by the Rev. Dr. Blaney—and a Sermon to recommend the revision of our present Version of the Bible by the Rev. Dr. White, Laudian professor of Arabic in the University of Oxford.

the Bible is the best standard of the English language. If this be fully ascertained, it must argue a presumption in me to offer the following sheets to the public. But in this, as in all other questions, it is necessary to state the matter with clearness and precision, instead of using vague and undefined terms. Do the advocates for this opinion mean, that our Translators have judiciously adopted many English words, in preference to those of a foreign growth? If this be the whole that is contended for, I will readily allow it, and bear the fullest testimony to the merit of our Translators; for it must needs be confessed, that our Version, in this respect, ought to be ranked among the standards of our language, if, in truth, the standard of a living language be capable of being ascertained. But to be *one* of the standards, and to be the *best* standard of it, are two things which are extremely different. Though the plain and simple turn of expression, which results from the choice of old English words, will intitle our Version to the former appellation, yet many other circumstances must be united to confirm its claim to the latter. It will be requisite therefore to submit to examination a few more questions upon this head. Are the words and phrases, employed by our Translators, generally placed in their proper order? Are they so arranged, as to preclude all obscurity and ambiguity? Do we always find the Antecedents, to which the Relatives refer? Hath a right attention been paid to the Modes and Times of Verbs? And is there a due propriety observed in the use of Particles, upon which the clearness of a sentence chiefly depends? I scarcely think, that any one will venture to answer in the affirmative; but unless these rules, or the greater part of them be complied with, I cannot possibly see, how our Version of the Bible, or any other composition,

sition, can lay claim to be called the *best* standard of a language. It is natural to imagine, that those who take opinions upon trust, and neglect the study of Grammar, should be affected with this popular prejudice; but that so excellent a critic, and so accurate a writer as Bishop Lowth should embrace the same sentiments, is matter of astonishment*; and indeed I should hardly have presumed to dissent from so great an authority, unless his Lordship himself had furnished me with the most decisive mode of confutation; for his Lordship has corrected many ungrammatical passages in our Version of the Old and New Testament; and the rules of criticism which he has laid down, and which are now as it were established, will enable us to correct several hundred errors of a similar nature in the New Testament alone.

It is possible, that disquisitions of this kind may appear to some readers more curious, than useful; and to others, to reflect a discredit upon religion, by exposing the faults of our Version. To those, who entertain so superstitious a reverence for it, as to think that it ought not to be controlled by the rules of Grammar, I will suggest two memorable facts, which may serve to strengthen their *pious prejudice.* There is extant a letter from Pope Gregory the Great to Desiderius a French Bishop, in which this Prelate is severely admonished for teaching Grammar: a crime of so enormous a magnitude, that it forced tears from the tender Pontif; and gave occasion to the following pathetic expostulation: " Quam rem ita molestè suscepimus, ac sumus vehementius aspernati, ut ea, quæ prius dicta fuerant, in gemitum et tristitiam verteremus; quia in uno se ore cum Jovis laudibus Christi laudes non capiunt.

---

* See the short introduction to English Grammar, p. 93. 2ᵈ. ed. where it is said " The Vulgar Translation of the Bible is the best standard of our language."

piunt *." In a letter to Bishop Leander, his Holyness discovers a more noble contempt of Grammar. The Exordium is truly solemn; and is dressed up with an elaborate pomp of words: "Non metacysmi collisionem fugio: non barbarismi confusionem devito: situs motusque et præpositionum casus servare contemno; quia indignum vehementer existimo, ut verba cœlestis oraculi restringam sub regulis Donati. †." If an elegant taste, and pure language be the marks of Heterodoxy, it is certain, that his Holyness most scrupulously avoided splitting upon so tremendous a rock.

But surely it would be misspending my own time, and that of my readers, to enter into a formal discussion of this subject. It is to be hoped, that the cloud of ignorance, which over-spread Europe for so many centuries, has been intirely dispelled by the learned and liberal inquiries of the past and present age. We may now affirm, without fearing the imputation of heresy, that the fine writings of antiquity are the best models upon which we can form ourselves, to improve both our taste and understanding: that the study of them is not only ornamental, but necessary to a Divine; and that Grammar is intitled to a distinguished place in his literary pursuits. In short, it may be admitted as a maxim, "that one of the most essential qualifications of a good translator, is to be a good grammarian; without which, all the theology of the Sorbonne will be of little use ‡." These are the expressions of a very acute, eloquent, and able writer, who is engaged in a most arduous and useful undertaking, for which he seems to be

B   eminently

* Lib. xi. Ep. 54.
† Lib. ii. Ep. 1. Cap. 5.
‡ See the Prospectus of a new translation of the Holy Bible by the Rev. Dr. Geddes, p. 141.

eminently qualified; and in whose success, not only every scholar, but every candid inquirer after truth must feel himself deeply interested.

CHAPTER II.

Upon Perspicuity.

AS Perspicuity is universally allowed to be the chief beauty of style, so of all requisites it is the most necessary in a Version of the Holy Scriptures. It is reasonably expected of every one who undertakes to translate a Heathen author, that he should have a competent knowledge of the language into which he translates; but were he to fall into a *few* inaccuracies of style, which are of little moment, and do not affect the drift and meaning of the sentence, we should be induced to ascribe them to a pardonable inadvertency; whereas if he should either misrepresent the sense of his author, or not make it clearly understood, he would scarcely be thought worthy of the least indulgence. Now if this be true in respect to a translation of the works of a Heathen writer, it may be applied in a much stronger degree to that of the Bible; for the former is designed only for those who have had the advantages of a liberal education; and it is frequently calculated rather for entertainment than for real use; whereas the latter is intended *to witness to the small and to the great*, and to be a perfect rule both of faith and manners.

The ambiguities in our Version, which are very numerous, and sometimes too gross to be defended, may be considered under the following heads:

I. It is often extremely difficult to find the Antecedents, to which the Relatives refer. Sometimes the Antecedents are so remote, that they cannot, consistently with the rules of English Grammar, belong to the supposed Relatives; and sometimes we can hardly distinguish any Antecedent at all. This perhaps may be thought to arise in a great measure from the nature of the English tongue. We use, for instance, the Pronoun *they* indiscriminately for things, and for persons of both sexes; whereas in almost all other languages, the Personal Pronouns are marked in the Plural, as well as in the Singular Number, by a distinction of Gender; which will often lead us to the knowledge of an Antecedent, that otherwise might not have been so easily discovered. It is true, that this may render it more difficult to write correctly in the English language; but that it is not an insuperable obstacle, we may learn from the example of our most approved authors. If this blemish were found in the works of Addison, Swift, and Middleton, they would not be admired by all those, who have a real taste for polite literature.

There was another circumstance very unfavourable to our Translators, as, in fact, it is to all who study the Scriptures; that is, the strange division into chapters and verses. It is not probable, that our Translators were authorized to new-model the Verses; but, in respect to the Chapters, it was ordered by James I. " that they should not be changed *without apparent necessity:*" a strong presumption, if not an undoubted proof, that some alterations were looked upon to be requisite. It is much to be lamented, that our Translators did not avail themselves of this permission; and, whether they judged it necessary to adhere to the present division, on account of the references made to it in all preceding commentaries; or whether we are to impute it to any other cause, it is certain, that they lost a fair opportunity to free us from an incumbrance, which has long afforded just grounds of complaint. But if they deemed it absolutely expedient to retain the present division of *all* the chapters, they ought to have inserted the regular Antecedent in the beginning of those, in which it was evidently deficient; and it seems the more surprizing, that they neglected it, because they themselves have borne testimony to the necessity, or, at least, to the propriety of admitting it; for they have furnished us with *two* instances (and *two* only throughout the four Evangelists, and the Acts of the Apostles) in which they have actually supplied it: namely, Luke XIX. 1. and John IX. 1. If it was necessary to supply this defect in *any* instance, was it not equally so in *all?* especially as the chapters above-mentioned have no peculiarity in them, which could require such an exclusive attention to be paid to them in preference to the rest. I cannot pass by this opportunity to remark, that among all the numerous Versions which I have hitherto examined, not one is to be found intirely free from this defect. Even that of L'Enfant and Beausobre, from whom we might with reason expect greater exactness, must necessarily be included in the same list. Had the Scriptures indeed been intended for the private perusal of the closet only, the reader would naturally have supplied the defect of the regular Antecedent by recurring to the preceding chapter. But as they are

appointed

appointed to be red in public, and that in detached parts, and to many among the hearers, who are not able to read; and as the tranflators muft have known, that they were employed in the work for this purpofe chiefly, one cannot but wonder that a *fingle* tranflator, one muft be aftonifhed to find that *every* tranflator, fhould be guilty of this neglect.—It is likewife no lefs remarkable, that the compilers of our Liturgy are chargeable with the fame inconfiftency in thofe felect portions of the Evangelifts, which are appointed for the Gofpels in the fervice of our Church. Among thefe there are about twenty in which the compilers have inferted the proper Antecedent; and in fome of them have modified the fenfe by the addition of feveral other words; while in an equal number at leaft they have omitted to infert even the proper Antecedent, though there appears no ground in either cafe on which fuch an inconfiftency of conduct can be juftified.

II. Another caufe of ambiguity in our prefent Verfion is the frequent ufe of equivocal expreffions. An unlettered reader is apt to be embaraffed by them; and is as likely to adopt the falfe, as the true meaning. I would not be underftood to intimate, that the fenfe is always neceffarily obfcured by words of doubtful fignification; but whether it be actually obfcured or not, it is the fame fault of language; for it is incumbent upon every one to exprefs himfelf with fo much precifion, that the terms employed by him cannot poffibly be mifapprehended. This was the opinion of one of the moft judicious authors of antiquity, who has left us admirable rules both for fpeaking and writing: " Vitanda in primis ambiguitas, non hæc folùm, quæ incertum intellectum facit, fed illa quoque, quæ, etiamfi turbare non poteft fenfum, in idem tamen verborum vitium incidit." And he farther declares in the same chapter: "Quare, non ut intelligere possit, sed ne omnino possit non intelligere, curandum est *."

III. A third cause of ambiguity is the indeterminate use of Prepositions. Our Translators seem often to have used them without considering whether they were well adapted to answer the purpose intended.

These imperfections in our present Version will be the subject of the three following chapters.

CHAPTER III.

Ambiguities occasioned by the Antecedents to which the Relatives refer, not being clearly distinguished.

Matth. III. 16.

"AND Jesus, when he was baptized, went up *straightway* [immediately] out of the water: and lo! the heavens were opened unto him, and *he* [John] saw the Spirit of God descending like a dove, and lighting upon him." It seems most probable, that *ude* refers to the Baptist, because it had been revealed unto him, that the visible descent of the Spirit would point out to him the Messiah. Accordingly we find the Substantive *John* inserted in many of our antient and modern English Versions; and indeed I am inclined to think with Mr. Wakefield, that

* Quinctil. Inst. lib. viii. § 2.

that αυτῳ likewife refers to the Baptift, unlefs it be confidered as a redundancy after the Hebrew idiom.

"*And feeing the multitudes* [When *Jefus* faw a great multitude of people] he went up *into a mountain* [a mountain] *and when he was fet* [and after he had fitten down] his difciples came unto him." This is the firft inftance in this Gofpel, where the want of an Antecedent occurs at the opening of a chapter. It has been fupplied by Wicklif*: " And *Jhefus* feynge the peple, went up into an hill &c." Our Tranflators have confounded in this, and in many other places, the Verb *to fit* with the Verb to *fet*, as it has been remarked by Bifhop Lowth †. Matth. V. 1.

"*Bleffed* [Happy] are ye when men fhall revile you, and perfecute you, and fhall fay all *manner* [kind] of evil againft you falfly for my fake: (12) Rejoyce, and be *exceeding* [exceedingly] glad, for great *is* [fhall be] your reward in heaven ; *for fo perfecuted they the prophets which were before you.*" It ought to be, " for thus the *teachers* were perfecuted, who were before you." Mr. Pilkington obferves upon this verfe : " Who perfecuted the Prophets? Not the men who reviled the Apoftles ; but, *They*, is a general Relative, and not improperly applied to the men of former times ‡." Mr. Pilkington has not expreffed himfelf here with his ufual accuracy and judgement ; for though the Pronoun *they* may be often applied to men in general, yet, in this inftance, it muft neceffarily refer to thofe who reviled the Apoftles, becaufe the 12th verfe is manifeftly connected with the 11th, therefore it is proper to make a little alteration in the words, and conftruction ———XI.

tion

---

* The tranflation by Wicklif, which I have ufed, was publifhed by Lewis at the end of his hiftory of the feveral Englifh tranflations of the Bible.

† Introduction to Englifh grammar, p. 80.

‡ Remarks upon feveral paffages of Scripture, &c. p. 99.

tion of the sentence, in order to prevent the possibility of a mistake.

Matth. VIII. 1. "*When he was come down* [While Jesus was coming down] from the mountain, great multitudes followed him." The regular Antecedent is in Wicklif: "But whanne *Jhesus* was come down fro the hill &c."

——IX. 1. "*And he entered into a ship* [Jesus went into a boat, or vessel] and passed over, and came into his own city." Here again Wicklif: "And *Jhesus* wente up into a boot, and passide over the watir &c."

——32. "As they went out, behold! *they* brought to him a dumb man possessed with the devil." One would imagine, that the blind men, who had just recovered their sight, had brought the demoniac; whereas they were gone away, and the people brought him. It should therefore be translated "After these men were departed, behold! *the people* brought to him a dumb man, who was a demoniac" Or, "a dumb man was brought to him" as Castalio renders it "allatus est ei mutus homo." After which manner is the Italian translation by Diodati: "Hor, come que' ciechi uscivano, ecco, gli fu presentato un huomo mutolo, indemoniato." Thus likewise Tyndal: "As they were come oute, beholde a dum man, possessed of a devil, was broughte too him."

——X. 1. "*And when he had called unto him his twelve disciples* [After Jesus had called together his twelve disciples] he gave them power *against* [over] unclean spirits to cast them out, and to heal *all manner of sickness, and all manner of disease* [every kind of disease, and every kind of infirmity.] It should be thus corrected in Matth. IV. 23. I have rendered νοσος by disease, and μαλακια by infirmity, upon the authority of Bishop Newcome, who with great

pro-

propriety obferves, that different words, which have nearly the fame fenfe, fhould be diftinguifhed in a tranflation, when the Englifh tongue furnifhes diftinct and proper terms*. Mr. Wakefield has tranflated νοσος and μαλακια in the fame manner. It is obfervable, that Tyndal fays, "and gave them power *over* uncleane fpirites" not "*againft*" as in our prefent Verfion.

"And behold! there was a man *which had his hand withered* [who had a withered hand] and they afked *him* [Jefus] faying, Is it lawful to heal on the fabbath-day? &c." As the text ftands in our Verfion, the queftion is not put to Jefus, but to the infirm man. It is not fo in Diodati: "ed effi fecero una domanda à *Gefù* dicendo &c." nor in L'Enfant and Beaufobre: "Les Pharifiens pour avoir lieu d'accufer *Jefus*, lui demanderent &c." — Matth. XII. 10.

"Then the Pharifees went out, and held a council againft *him* [Jefus] how they might deftroy him." The infirm man is mentioned laft in the preceding verfe; fo that, according to our Tranflation, the Pharifees confpired againft *him*, not againft *Jefus*. —— 14.

"The Pharifees *alfo with the Sadducees* [and the Sadducees] came, *and tempting, defired him that he would fhew them a fign from heaven* [and defired *Jefus* to fhew them a fign from heaven, in order to tempt, or, to try him."] The beginning of this verfe is ftrangely rendered by Mr. Purver: "Whither fome Pharifees and Sadducees came &c." — XVI. 1.

"Pilate faid unto them, ye have a *watch*, go your way, make it as fure as you can. (66) So they went, and made the fepulchre fure, fealing the ftone, and fetting a watch." Though the 65th verfe is a complete fentence, yet it cannot be underftood, unlefs we take along with it the verfe immediately preceding or follow- — XXVII. 65.

---

* Preface to the improved Verfion, &c. of the twelve minor prophets, p. xxvii.

following; for our Translators intended, that the Pronoun *it*, which is in Italic characters, should refer to *sepulchre*, whereas the rules of construction require, that it should refer to *watch*. This is doubtless an inaccuracy. Now if we put the Substantive instead of the Pronoun in the 65th, and insert the Pronoun in the 66th verse, there will be no ambiguity: " Pilate said unto them, Take a *guard*, go, and make the *sepulchre* as *secure* as you can. (66) And they went, and *secured it, setting a seal* upon the stone, and *appointing a guard*." The sense is very clear in Tyndal: " Pilate sayed unto them, Take watchmen, go, and make it as sure as ye can; and they wente, and made the sepulchre sure with watchmen, and sealed the stone." Κυστωδια is likewise rendered " watchmen" in Coverdale's, and in Mathew's Bibles.

Mark I. 42. " And soon as he had spoken, *immediately the leprosy departed from him* [the leprosy immediately departed from *the man*] and he was cleansed: (43) *And he straightly* [And *Jesus* strictly] charged him, and *forthwith* [instantly] sent him away." No ambiguity in this kind appears either in Beza or Schmidius: they both translate it, " Et graviter interminatus est ei *Jesus*" and the version of Mons is equally clear: " *Jesus* le renvoya aussi-tost, &c*." Thus also Diodati: " E *Gesù*, havendogli fatti severi divieti, lo mandò prestamente via." We find the regular Antecedent repeated by Wicklif: " And *Jhesus* thretanyde him, and anoon *Jhesus* putte hym out, &c." This repetition had much better have been avoided.

—— II. 1. " *And again he entered* [*Jesus* entered again] into Capernaum, after

---

* This Version was made by a doctor of the Sorbonne, and first printed at Mons 1666. Within two years after the publication six impressions were sold.

after some days, and it was *noised* [heard, or understood] that he was in the house." I do not see, that ηκεσθη implies more than this; and " noised" is undoubtedly a very vulgar expression. It is in the Rhemish translation of the N. T. " and it was *heard* that he was in the house †."

" *And he* [Jesus] entered again into the synagogue, *and there was a man there which* [where was a man who] had a withered hand : (2) *And they watched him* [and *the Pharisees* watched *Jesus*] whether he would heal him on the sabbath-day, &c." After this manner L'Enfant and Beausobre : " *Jesus* étant entré dans une synagogue, il s'y trouva un homme qui avoit une main seche : (2) Et *les Pharisiens* observoient *Jesus* pour voir, &c."   Mark III. 1.

" *And he began again to teach by the sea-side* [*Jesus* began to teach again by the side of the lake] and there was gathered *unto* [about] him a great multitude, *so that he entered into a ship, and sat in the sea*, &c. [so that he went into a boat, and sat *in it* upon the lake]." So Diodati : " montato in navicella, sedeva *in essa* nel mare." Mr. Markland very properly connects εις το πλοιον with εν τη θαλασση, and Mr. Bowyer in his excellent edition of the N. T. has put καθησθαι between commas : " ὡςε αυτον εμβαντα εις το πλοιον, καθησθαι, εν τη θαλασση."   —— IV. 1.

" But without a parable *spake he* [he spake] not unto *them* ; and when *they* were alone, he expounded all things to his disciples." It should be, " and expounded all things to his disciples, when they were alone " or rather " in private." If we do not alter the order of the words, the Pronoun *they* must refer to *them*, that is, the multitude ; which is quite foreign to the meaning of the Evangelist.   —— — 34.

† The first edition of the Rhemish N. T. translated by the Papists was printed at Rheims 1582. That which I have quoted was printed at Antwerp 1600.

Some of our oldest Versions are free from this inaccuracy. Thus Wicklif: " And he spak not to hem withoute parable, but he expownede to hise disciplis alle thingis bi hemsilf." Thus also Coverdale: " And without parables spake he nothinge unto them; but unto his disciples he expounded all thynges privately " and to the same purport is the Geneva Bible †: " but he expounded all things to his disciples apart."

Mark V. 1. " *And they came over* [Jesus and his disciples went over] unto the other side of the *sea* [lake] into the country of the Gadarenes. (2) And when *he* was come out of the *ship* [boat] &c." Here we see, that in the two first verses of a chapter there are two Relatives without any Antecedents. But all is cleared up by rendering the first verse " Jesus and his disciples, &c."

—— VI. 1. " *And he went out from thence* [Jesus departed from Capernaum] and came into his own *country* [city] &c." I have followed Dr. Owen in rendering πατρίδα by " city" viz. the city of Nazareth.

—— — 53. " And when they had passed over, they came into the land of Gennesaret, *and drew to the shore* [and put to shore:] (54) And when they were come out of the *ship* [boat] *straightway they knew him.*" Who knew him? The disciples, according to our Version; yet it is certain, that the Evangelist does not mean them. It ought to be " the inhabitants of those parts, or, that place, immediately knew him." We see in Wetstein (what has not escaped Bishop Pearce) that οἱ ἄνδρες τε τοπε, and τε τοπε εκεινε are found in several MSS. which probably gave occasion to Beza to render it: " homines loci illius " and likewise to Diodati: " subito

---

† The Geneva Bible was translated by the English refugees in Queen Mary's reign, among whom was Bishop Coverdale. I have made use of the first edition which was printed at Geneva by Rowland Hall in 1560.

bito la gente lo riconobbe." Thus also the author of the Version of Mons, " et ceux de ce lieu-là" and L'Enfant and Beausobre " ceux du païs." It is remarkable, that all our Versions, from Wicklif down to Wynne, are faulty in this instance. One would think, that the parallel passage in Matth. xiv. 35. were sufficient by itself to point out the true meaning.

"*Then came together unto him the Pharisees, and certain of the Scribes, which came from Jerusalem* [The Pharisees, and some of the Scribes, who had come from Jerusalem, resorted together to *Jesus.*]   Mark VII. 1.

" And *straightway* [immediately] his ears were opened, and the string of his tongue was loosed, and he spake *plain* [plainly.] (36) And *he* [Jesus] charged them that they should tell no man; but the more he charged them, so much the more *a great deal* [abundantly] they published it." The regular Antecedent is inserted by Diodati: " E *Gesù* ordinò loro, &c." and likewise by L'Enfant and Beausobre : " Et *Jesus* leur défendit d'en rien dire à personne."   ——— 35.

" *And he said unto them,* [Jesus said unto *the people, and his disciples*] Verily I say unto you, that there *be some of them that stand here which shall not taste of death* [are some here present who shall not die] till they have seen the kingdom of God come with power." Grotius, Dr. Clarke, and others rightly observe, that this verse belongs to the foregoing discourse; and ought not to have been separated from the former chapter. We find it actually joined to it in the Versions of Wicklif, Tyndal, Coverdale, and L'Enfant and Beausobre.   —— IX. 1.

" *And he arose from thence, and cometh into the coasts* [Jesus departed   —— X. 1.

parted from *Galilee*, and came unto the borders] of Judæa, by the farther side of *Jordan* [the river Jordan &c.]

Mark XI. 1. " *And when they came nigh* [When *Jesus and his disciples* were come nigh] to Jerusalem, unto Bethphage, and Bethany at the *mount of Olives* [foot of the mount of olives] he *sendeth forth* [sent] two of his disciples, (2) and *saith* [said] unto them, Go *your way* [Go] into the village over-against you; and as soon as ye *be entered* [enter] into it, ye *shall* [will] find a colt tied, *whereon never man sat, loose him, and bring him* [on which no man ever sat: loose *it* and bring *it hither*.] The same strange inaccuracy occurs in the 7th verse of this chapter, and in Luke xix. 30. Why did not our Translators follow Coverdale, who has rendered it " loose *it* and bringe *it hyther*."

—— XII. 1. " *And he began* [Jesus began] to speak unto *them* [*the chief priests, and the scribes, and the elders*] by parables &c." Wicklif has inserted but one Antecedent: " And *Jhesus* bigan to speke to hem in parablis &c."

—— XIII. 1. " *And as he went out* [While *Jesus* was going out] of the temple, one of his disciples *saith* [said] unto him, Master, see what *manner* [kind] of stones, and what buildings are here."

—— — 28. " Now learn a parable *of* [from] the fig-tree: when *her* [its] branch is yet tender, and putteth forth leaves, ye know that summer is near: (29) So ye in like manner, when ye shall see these things *come* [coming] to pass, know *that it is nigh*, even at the door." What is nigh? The Evangelist cannot mean to say again, that summer is nigh; and yet these words import it. The Version of Zurich inserts " regnum dei " * and the Geneva, and

---

* This Latin Version by Leon de Juda was printed at Zurich 1579; and is commonly called Versio Tigurina.

and the Bishops-Bible † have " the kingdom of God is near."
We should either render it so with these Versions; or " the coming of the Son of man is nigh;" after which manner Schmidius:
" scitote prope esse ad fores adventum filii hominis." Glassius has quoted Matth. xxiv. 33. (where is the same ellipsis) and has explained it by the following Canon, " Relativum pronomen non raro deest in Hebræo V. cum Græco N. T. textu *." This is undoubtedly true; but an English translator should consider, that what makes good Hebrew or Greek, may often make very bad English.

" After two days was the feast of the Passover, and of unleavened bread: and the chief priests, and the scribes sought how they might take *him by craft* [*Jesus* by subtilty] and put him to death." — Mark XIV. 1.

" And they led Jesus away to the high priest; *and with him* [with whom] were assembled all the chief priests, and the scribes, and the elders." Though the high priest is the immediate Antecedent, yet the sentence is made clearer by this alteration. Thus Beza: " Tunc abduxerunt Jesum ad pontificem maximum, cum quo convenerunt &c." —— 53.

" *And when the sabbath day was past* [After the sabbath was past] Mary Magdalene, and Mary the mother of James, and Salome, had bought sweet spices, that they might *come* [go] and anoint *him*" Whom? James is the Antecedent. It ought to be translated " and anoint *Jesus*" or " *the body of Jesus.*" Thus the Vulgate: " ut venientes ungerent *Jesum*" and Wicklif, who professes to render from the Vulgate, has the same: " to come and — XVI. 1.

to

---

† I have made use of the first edition of the Bishops-Bible printed in 1568.
* Philologia sacra canon xxii. p. 339. ed. Amst. 1711.

to enoynte *Jhesus*." Thus likewise the Version of Mons " pour venir embaumer *Jesus*" and Diodati, and L'Enfant and Beausobre, in the like manner.

Mark XVI. 18.
" They shall lay hands on the sick, *and they* [who] shall recover."——But might it not be translated " and the sick shall recover by the imposition of their hands." If this should not be thought literal enough, I would rather render it here, and in all similar passages " put their hands upon them " for " *laying hands upon* " is an equivocal expression; and often denotes an act of violence, as it appears from many places both in the O. and N. T.

Luke V. 1.
" *And it came to pass*, that as the people pressed upon him [While the people pressed upon *Jesus*] to hear the word of God, he stood by the lake of Gennesareth."

———17.
" *And it came to pass* on a certain day as he was teaching, that there were Pharisees and doctors of the law sitting by, *which* were come from every town of Galilee, and Judæa, *and Jerusalem*, and the power of the Lord was present to heal *them*." Dr. Macknight observes in his very useful essay, that the Relative Pronoun αυτες in this verse, refers not to the Pharisees, and doctors of the law, who are just before mentioned, but to such sick people as were in the crowd; agreeably to the use of Relative Pronouns *. This may be true in respect to a *Greek* Relative Pronoun; but an *English* one must necessarily refer to the nearest, and not to a remote Antecedent. We should therefore render εις το ιασθαι αυτες " to heal those who had diseases." The author of

---

* Essay iv. on translating the Greek language used by the writers of the N. T. p. 49.—Mr. Pilkington in his Remarks &c. p. 99. quotes Luke v. 17. and seems to have too hastily defended the indeterminate use of Pronouns in the English language.

of the Version of Mons has avoided any obscurity : " la vertu du Seigneur agissoit pour la guerison *des malades*." So likewise L'Enfant and Beausobre: " la vertu du Seigneur se déploya dans la guerison *des malades*." And Wicklif has judiciously departed from the Vulgate on this occasion : " And the vertu of the Lord was to heele *syk men*."—Perhaps it would not be improper to place a colon after νομοδιδασκαλοι, and to read with the Cambridge MS. ησαν δε εληλυθοτες &c. in which case this verse might be thus rendered : " While *Jesus* was teaching on a certain day, *several* Pharisees, and doctors of the law were sitting by : *and there were also those* who came out of every town of Galilee, and Judæa, and *from* Jerusalem; and the power of the Lord was present to heal them."

" *And it came to pass on the second sabbath after the first he* [Upon the second sabbath after the first, *Jesus*] went through the corn-fields; and his disciples plucked the ears of corn, &c."   Luke VI. 1.

" And Judas the brother of James, and Judas Iscariot, *which*   — — 16. [who] also was the traitor. (17) And *he* [Jesus] came down with them, and stood in the plain."—Beza and some others have placed a parenthesis from ver. 14. to the end of ver. 16. making the construction και εκλεξαμενος,—και καταβας;—ιςη. This has been adopted by the translators of the Geneva Bible.—Another method has been followed by L'Enfant and Beausobre: " (16) et Judas Iscariot, qui fut celui qui livra *Jesus*. (17) Ensuite étant descendu avec eux &c." Here it is not necessary to put the proper Antecedent in the 17th, because it is inserted in the 16th verse, and prevents any ambiguity. I leave it to the reader to determine which of these three interpretations is the best. It is manifest, that any of them is preferable to that in our present

Verſion; which obliges us to ſeek a remote Antecedent, though there are ſeveral Antecedents immediately preceding.

Luke VII. 1.
"*Now when he had ended all his ſayings in the audience* [After Jeſus had ended his diſcourſe in the hearing] of the people, he entered into Capernaum."

— — 15. "And he *that* [who] was dead, ſat up, and began to ſpeak; and *he* [Jeſus] delivered him to his mother." It is ſtill more obſcure in the Vulgate: "Et reſedit qui erat mortuus, et cœpit loqui; et dedit illum matri ſuæ." In the Verſion of Mons, and in L'Enfant and Beauſobre, the regular Antecedent is inſerted "Jeſus le rendit à ſa mere."

— — 29. "And all the people that heard *him*, and the publicans, juſtified God, being baptized with the baptiſm of John." Our Tranſlators have added *him* in an improper place, which makes the ſentence ambiguous; for the people are thereby repreſented hearing the publicans, as well as Jeſus; a fault, which occurs in the Spaniſh Verſion: "Y todo el pueblo oyendo *lo*, y los publicanos, juſtificaron à Dios, baptizandoſe con el baptiſmo de Joan †." Our Tranſlators have evidently copied after the Biſhops-Bible, inſtead of following Cranmer's, which was more accurate: "And all the people, and the publicans that herde hym, juſtified God &c." The expreſſion "juſtifying God" ſhould be uſed however with great caution; eſpecially as it is not very eaſily underſtood by the lower ranks of men. Perhaps this verſe might be better rendered thus: "And all the people, and the publicans who heard him, thankfully acknowledged the juſtice" or "mercy of God, and were baptized with the baptiſm of John." In the

---

† This is cited from the tranſlation by Cypriano de Valera, the ſecond edition of which was printed at Amſterdam 1602, and which I have uſed.

the Verſion of Mons, εδικαιωσαν τον Θεον is rendered " ont fecondé le deſſein de Dieu" which is not only an unwarrantable deviation from the Original, but is ſubverſive of the true meaning of the paſſage.

"*And it came to paſs afterward that he* [*Jeſus* afterward] went throughout every city and village preaching and *ſhewing* [publiſhing] the glad tidings of the kingdom of God, and the twelve were with him."   Luke VIII. 1.

"*Then he* [*Jeſus*] called his twelve diſciples together, and gave them power and authority over all *devils* [demons] and to cure diſeaſes."   —— IX. 1.

"While he thus ſpake, there came a cloud, and overſhadowed *them:* and *they* feared, as *they* entered into the cloud." This verſe ſeems thoroughly confuſed by theſe Pronouns. It had better be rendered "and *the diſciples* were afraid, *when they ſaw* them entering into the cloud." So L'Enfant and Beauſobre: "et les diſciples furent ſaiſis de frayeur *en les voyant* entrer dans la nueé." Caſtalio has thrown the latter part of the 33d verſe into the 34th, and has rendered the whole very clearly: "Hæc eo loquente, et quid diceret neſciente, extitit nubes quæ illos obumbravit. Quibus in nubem ingreſſis, quum hi territi eſſent &c."   —— 34.

"*And it came to paſs, that as he* [As *Jeſus*] was praying in a certain place, *when he had ceaſed* [after he had made an end] one of his diſciples ſaid unto him, Lord, teach us to pray, as *John alſo* [John] taught his diſciples."   —— XI. 1.

"In the mean time, when there were gathered together an innumerable multitude of people, inſomuch that they trode one upon another, *he began to ſay unto his diſciples firſt of all, Beware ye of the leaven of the Phariſees* [*Jeſus* ſaid unto his diſciples, Above all   —— XII. 1.

all things beware of the leaven of the Pharisees] which is hypocrisy." I have followed Beza, Wetstein, and Bowyer in joining πρωτον with προσεχετε, and not with τες μαθητας αυτε. Thus Tyndal: "First of all beware of the leven of Pharisees &c." and in the like manner Coverdale, Mathew, Tavener, and Archbishop Parker. The three last words, viz. ἥτις ἐςιν ὑποκρισις are with reason thought by Bishop Pearce and Dr. Owen to be an interpolation.

Luke XIII. 1.
"There were present at that *season some that told him of* [time some persons who informed *Jesus* concerning] the Galilæans, whose blood Pilate had mingled with their sacrifices."

—— XIV. 1.
"*And it came to pass, as he went* [After *Jesus* had entered] into the house of one of the *chief* [ruling] Pharisees to eat bread on the sabbath-day, they watched him." This is the meaning of εν τω ελθειν εις οικον, and accordingly Beza and Schmidius render it "quum venisset in domum." So Wicklif: "hade entrid" and the Geneva Bible: "when he was entred." Bishop Pearce remarks, that τινος των αρχοντων των φαρισαιων should be translated "one of the ruling Pharisees" that is, who was a ruler among the Jews, and a Pharisee too.

—— — 2.
"And behold! *there was a certain man before him which had the dropsy.*" It should be "there was before him a certain man who had the dropsy." The transposing of these words makes the meaning very different. Nothing can be more curious than the rendering by Purver: "When behold there was some man *before him* that had the dropsy *before him.*"

—— XV. 1.
"*Then drew near unto him all the publicans and sinners for to hear him.*" "[Several of the publicans and sinners drew near unto

Jesus

Jesus to hear him."] Παντες signifies here not *all*, but *several*, as in many places in the N. T.

"And he went, and joined himself to a citizen of that country; *and he* [who] sent him into his fields to feed swine." It surprizes me, that Mr. Wynne has translated και επεμψεν " *and he sent*" as it is in our present Version. Και supplies here the place of the Pronoun Relative ὁς, as in Mark XVI. 18. above-mentioned; and likewise in many passages in the N. T. as it has been observed by Dr. Macknight*; but king James's translators do not appear to have considered the variety of senses in which the particle και is used. Most of our early translators were more knowing in this respect. Thus Tyndal in Luke XV. 15. " *which* sente him to his fielde to keepe his swine," and Coverdale: " *which* sent hym to hys feldes to kepe swyne" and Mathew and Taverner in the same manner. The Vulgate has *et misit*, but Beza and the Zurich Version have *qui misit*.

"*And he said also* [*Jesus* said] to his disciples, There was a certain rich man *which* [who] had a steward &c."

"*Then said he unto the disciples* [*Jesus* said to *his* disciples] it is impossible but that offences will come &c." We find μαθητας αυτε in several MSS. which seems to be the best reading; and which is adopted in the Geneva Bible.

"*And he spake a parable unto them, to this end, that men ought always to pray, and not to faint:* [*Jesus* spake a parable to *his disciples, to teach them,* that *they* ought *frequently* to pray, and not to despond." I have rendered αυτοις " to his disciples" in conformity to Mr. Markland; and παντοτε " frequently" in conformity to Bishop Pearce, and to Dr. Macknight who says, that παντοτε has the

Luke XV. 15.

——— XVI. 1.

——— XVII. 1.

———XVIII. 1.

* Essay iv. p. 59.

the same meaning in John XVIII. 20 *. The first eight verses of this chapter, as Mr. Markland observes, depend upon what went before, and should not have been detached from it by a new chapter.

Luke XXI. 1. "*And he looked up* [Jesus looked up] *and saw rich men casting their gifts into the treasury* &c."

——XXIII. 1. "*And the whole multitude of them arose, and led him unto Pilate.*" Here are two Relatives without an Antecedent at the beginning of a chapter. It is rendered by L'Enfant and Beausobre : "Ensuite toute l'assemblée se leva, et ayant conduit Jesus chez Pilate &c." But the common people are not included in the πληθος αυτων, as Dr. Owen observes, which ought to lead us to translate it more distinctly : "All the elders, and the chief priests, and the scribes arose, and led *Jesus* to Pilate."

——XXIV. 1. "*Now upon the first day* [Upon the first day] *of the week, very early in the morning, they came unto the sepulchre, bringing the spices which they had prepared, and certain others with them.*" It would be much clearer thus : "*the women, who had followed Jesus from Galilee*, came to the sepulchre—*and there were some* others with them." The Antecedent is supplied in the Version of Mons, though not perhaps fully enough : "Mais le premier jour de la semaine *ces femmes*, & quelques autres avec elles, vinrent au sepulchre &c." Bengelius says, that the latter end of the preceding chapter ought to be added to this : "They rested on the sabbath ; but, on the first day of the week, brought spices &c."

—— 5. "And as *they* [the women] were afraid, and bowed down their faces to the earth, *they* [the men] said unto them, Why seek ye the living among the dead ?" As they were called *men* in the preceding

---

* Harmony, p. 428. second edition.

ceding verse, from the shape assumed by them, I should rather supply the ellipsis by *men*, though they are stiled *Angels* ver. 23.

" And behold! *two of them* [two of *his disciples*] went that same day to a village called Emmaus &c." There is no Antecedent in the preceding verse. Luk.XXIV. 13.

" Yea and certain women also of our company made *us* astonished, which were early at the sepulchre." It ought to be rendered: " Yea, and some women also of our company, who were early at the sepulchre, astonished us." This fault runs throughout almost all the English Versions; but Purver's is indisputably the worst in this instance: " Nay, and some women *of us* made us amazed, who were in the morning at the grave." ——— 22.

" *And they told what things were done in the way* [And *the two disciples* related what had passed upon the road] and *how* [that] he was known *of* [by] them *in breaking of bread* [in *the* breaking of bread" or, " in breaking bread." It is necessary to mark likewise here the two disciples, because the eleven, and those who were with them, had been just speaking of the resurrection of Jesus—I cannot forbear mentioning, that Wicklif has not fallen into the inaccuracy, of which king James's translators were guilty; for he properly renders it " in *the* brekinge of bred." ——— 35.

" *One of the two which heard John speak, and followed him, was Andrew Simon Peter's brother.*" There is no other than John, to whom *him* can have a reference; and yet we find in the foregoing verse, that it was not John, but Jesus, whom the two disciples had followed. We ought therefore to translate it thus: " One of the two, who *had* heard the testimony given by John, and *had* followed *Jesus*, was Andrew Simon Peter's brother." There is no ambiguity in Tyndal: " One of the two which heard John speake, John I. 40.

speake, and folowed *Jesus*, was Andrew Simon Peter's brother." Nor in Castalio : " Erat Andreas Simonis Petri frater unus ex duobus, qui cum audito Johanne secuti fuerant." Nor in Diodati : " Andrea, fratello di Simon Pietro, era uno de' due, ch' aveano udito quel ragionamento da Giovanni, ed aveano seguitato Gesù." And the French Versions are equally clear.

John II. 2. " *And both Jesus was called, and his disciples* [And Jesus, and his disciples also were invited] to the marriage: (3) *And when they wanted wine.*" Does not this indicate, that Jesus and his disciples wanted wine? I have not met with this ambiguity in any other Version whatever. Wicklif renders it " And whanne wijn failide " in which he has been followed by almost all our translators ; and nothing can be more close to the Original, ὑστερησαντος οινȣ. Bishop Pearce observes, " that this want of wine might have been occasioned by their having more company on the two preceding days, and on this third day, than the bridegroom and bride expected." It grieves me to see a respectable Prelate so eminently trifling. It is by a very few injudicious notes in this kind, that an elaborate and useful commentary has been brought into disrepute.

— III. 23. " And John also was baptizing in Enon, near to Salim, because there was much water there ; *and they came* [and many persons came] and were baptized." The disciples of Jesus were mentioned in the foregoing verse, to whom the Pronoun *they* must refer according to the rules of grammar ; yet it is probable, that Jesus and his disciples were then at some distance from John ; and, in fact, we find, that Jesus was then employed in baptizing, that is, by the ministry of his disciples. Castalio is very clear on this head : " ventitabantque *homines*, et baptizabantur "

and

and fo is Schimidius: " veniebant eò *homines*, et baptizabantur." And it is to the same purport in the French and Italian Versions. The bulk of the English translators were probably misled by the rendering in Beza and the Vulgate: " veniebant et baptizabantur."

" When therefore *the Lord* knew how the Pharisees had heard, John IV. 1. that *Jesus* made and baptized more disciples than John." This seems to be one of the strangest renderings in the N. T. for the words " *the Lord knew*" must be thought by the bulk of readers to mean, that " *God knew*" which is far from the scope of the Sacred writer. Of all the Latin translators, Tremellius has best rendered it ; " Cognovit autem *Jeschua*, quod audiverunt Pharisæi, quod discipulos multos faceret, et baptizaret plus quam Juchanan." This is the true sense, though very harshly expressed. In the Version of Mons there is great propriety : " *Jesus* donc ayant sçu que les Pharisiens avoient appris, qu' *il* faisoit plus de disciples, & baptizoit plus de personnes que Jean " and this interpretation, which differs not from that in Tremellius, receives additional credit from Dr. Owen, who advises us to read ὁ Ιησυς for ὁ Κυριος, and ὁτι αυτος for ὁτι Ιησυς ; the first reading being supported by several MSS. and the second by some of the most antient Versions. Our English translation will then stand thus : " As soon as *Jesus* knew that the Pharisees had heard, that *he* had made more disciples, and baptized more persons than John." Wicklif has rendered it in the following manner : " Therefore as *Jhesus* knew that the Farisees herden, that *Jhesus* makith and baptisith more discyplis than Jon." This is copied from the Vulgate, in which the noun *Jesus* is repeated instead of using the Pronoun, agreeably to the practice of

E the

the writers of the O. and N. T. of which Glassius has given several instances *; but it is certain, that the repetition of the Noun or Substantive produces a very unpleasing effect in the English language.

John VII. 45. "Then came the officers to the chief priests and Pharisees: *and they* [who] said unto them, Why have ye not brought him?" The Zurich Version hath " *qui* dixerunt iis" and L'Enfant and Beausobre, " *qui* leur ayant demandé."

—VIII. 24. "I said therefore unto you, that ye shall die in your sins; for if ye believe not that I am *he*, ye shall die in your sins." Grotius observes upon this passage " Ubi εγω ειμι simpliciter ponitur, intelligendum est de quo ante agebatur. Sic infra xviii. 5. subauditur Jesus. Hic vero lux mundi." We may therefore render it, " *I am the light of the world*" but should it not be thought proper to go so far back as the 12th verse, in which Jesus thus calls himself, we may translate it, " *I am from above*" or " *I am not of this world*," which expressions are used in the preceding verse. Any of these three interpretations is better than what we find in our Version; where the Pronoun *he* is injudiciously added, as there is no Antecedent.

—IX. 22. " *These words spake his parents* [His parents spake these words] because they feared the Jews; for the Jews had agreed already, that if any man did confess that *he* was Christ, he should be put out of the synagogue." This verse, like the foregoing, is obscured by the Pronoun *he*. It ought to be " if any man confessed that *Jesus* was the Christ &c." Thus the Version of Mons: " que quiconque reconnoistroit *Jesus* pour estre le Christ &c." and L'Enfant and Beausobre: " que si quelqu'un reconnoissoit *Jesus* pour

---

* Philologia sacra canon xii. p. 376.

pour le Meſſie &c."—— Another inſtance in this kind occurs in Acts XII. 25. "*And as John fulfilled* [And while John was fulfilling] his courſe, he ſaid, *Whom think ye* [Who do you think] that I am? I am not *he* [the Chriſt.] But behold! there cometh one after me, *whoſe ſhoes of his feet* [the ſhoes of whoſe feet] I am not worthy to looſe." The Pronoun *he*, inſerted in the text by way of ſupplement, throws no more light upon this, than upon the paſſages juſt mentioned. It is rendered by Schmidius: "Non ſum is ego quem putatis" conformably to the Vulgate: " Quem me arbitramini eſſe non ſum ego." And this has been followed by Coverdale: " I am not he that ye take me for" and alſo by Archbiſhop Cranmer: " Whom ye think that I am, the ſame am I not."

" Then when Jeſus came, he found, *that he had lien in the grave four days already* [that *Lazarus* had already lain in the grave four days]." Though this is ſo remarkable a circumſtance, that it cannot be ſuſpected that the moſt ignorant reader could be miſled, yet, for the ſake of accuracy, Lazarus ought to be particularly named, becauſe he had not been mentioned in the preceding verſe. Scarcely any tranſlators, except Diodati, and L'Enfant and Beauſobre were aware of this: " Geſù adunque venuto trovò, che *Lazaro* era già da quattro giorni nel monumento"—" que *Lazare* étoit dans le tombeau." John XI. 17.

" *And when the day* [When the day] of Penteсoſt was fully come, *they were all* [all the *Apoſtles* were] with one accord in one place." Beza ſays, that οἱ Ἀπόστολοι is in two MSS. but, without laying any ſtreſs upon them, I think, we ought to render it ſo, not only becauſe the Apoſtles were mentioned in the laſt verſe of Acts II. 1.

the preceding chapter, but becaufe many think it probable, that the Apoftles only were in that place.

Acts II. 41. "Then they *that* [who] gladly received his word, were baptized; and the fame day there were added *unto them* about three thoufand *fouls*." It is here faid, that this number was added to thofe who had been baptized; whereas St. Luke means, that there were added *to the difciples*, or, *to the Church*, about three thoufand *perfons*. Thus the Zurich Verfion: "addita funt *Ecclefiæ*" and the Spanifh Verfion: "y fueron añedidas *á la Iglefia*" and L'Enfant and Beaufobre: "et *l'Eglife* s' augmenta ce jour là d'environ trois mille perfonnes." The Geneva Bible printed by Barker 1756 reads in this place, "and the fame day there were added *to the Church* about three thoufand foules." Had our Tranflators omitted the words "*unto them*" which they took from the Bifhops-Bible, and which are not in the Original, they would not have fallen into this error. The Vulgate is clear without any addition: "Et appofitæ funt in die illa animæ circiter tria millia" and fo is Caftalio, who writes with a little more terfenefs: "Et accefferunt eo die hominum capita ad tria millia" and after the fame manner Diodati: "ed in quel giorno furono aggiunte intorno di tremila perfone." It is very remarkable, that this verfe feems to be rendered more accurately by Wicklif, than by any of the Englifh tranflators: "Thanne thei that refleyden his word weren baptized, and in that day foulis weren encreefid about three thoufynde."

———III. 16. "And his name, through faith in his name, hath made this man ftrong, whom ye now fee and know; yea, *the faith which is by him*, hath given him this perfect foundnefs in the prefence of you

you all." The promiscuous use of *his* and *him* has greatly darkened this verse; but it will be sufficiently clear, if we put the Substantive instead of the Pronoun in one place: " yea, the faith which is by *Christ*," or rather " *in Christ*."

" But those things which God before had shewed by the mouth of all his prophets, that Christ should suffer, he hath so fulfilled." Acts III. 18. In this verse the Antecedent to *he* is ambiguous: it certainly is *God*; but, in the translation, it rather appears to be *Christ*. The Original has no obscurity in it, and might have been rendered thus: " But God hath thus fulfilled those things which he had before declared by the mouth of all his prophets &c." The words παθειν τον Χριςον are said in Curcellæus's edition to be omitted in some Greek copies; and Grotius says, " Subdubitari potest, an hæ voces sint pars sensus, an glossema additum; quia desunt in vetere illo manuscripto." Perhaps it would be better to leave them out.

" And as *they* spake [While *Peter and John* were speaking] unto the people, the priests and the *captain of the temple* [commander of the guard of the temple] and the Sadducees *came* [came suddenly] upon them." —— IV. 1.

" And when they had set *them* [the two Apostles] in the midst, they asked, By what power, or by what name have ye done this?" —— — 7. According to our translation, they set in the midst no fewer than five thousand converts; and this gross inaccuracy is in all the Versions which I have examined, except the French and Italian: L'Enfant and Beausobre say " E ayant fait venir devant eux *Pierre et Jean*" and Diodati: " E fatti comparir quivi in mezzo *Pietro e Giovanni*, domandarono loro &c."

" And when *they* had heard *that*, they *lift* up their voices to God with —— — 24.

with one accord, and said, Lord &c." The immediate Antecedent of *they* is Peter and John; but, as soon as they were dismissed from the council, they related the whole transaction to the other ten, who offered up this prayer. We ought therefore to render it " And after *the other ten*" or " *the rest of the Apostles* had heard *it*, they *lifted* up their voices to God &c."

Acts VI. 6. " Whom they set before the Apostles; *and when they had prayed* [who, after they had prayed] *they laid* [put] their hands on them." In the Vulgate the ambiguity is still greater: " Hos statuerunt ante conspectum Apostolorum; et orantes imposuerunt eis manus." How much better is the Zurich Version? " Quos statuerunt coram Apostolis, *qui* cum orassent, imposuerunt eis manus." The Spanish Version also is here free from any defect. " A estos presentaron en presencia de los Apostoles, *los quales* orando les pusieron las manos en encima."

—— VII. 1. " Then said the high priest, Are these things so? (2) And *he* [Stephen] said, Men, *brethren* [Brethren] and fathers, hearken." It is very extraordinary, that our Translators should omit mentioning Stephen's name at the beginning of this chapter, since it does not occur before the 59th verse, or the last but one; so that the common people must hear the whole chapter, before they know who is the speaker; but extraordinary as this may appear, I see no exception to it in any English translation, except in that by Wicklif: " And the prince of prestis seide to *Stevene* whether these thingis han hem so?"

—— — 4. " Then came he out of the land of the Chaldæans, and dwelt in Charran; and *from thence* [thence] when his father was dead, *he* [God] removed him into this land wherein ye now dwell. (5) *And he gave him none* [But he gave him no] inheritance in it."

Both

Both Laurence Tomfon's Bible*, and the Geneva Bible fay "*God brought him*" and L'Enfant and Beaufobre render it "*Dieu le fit paſſer.*"

"And delivered him out of all his afflictions, and gave him favour and wiſdom in the ſight of Pharaoh king of Egypt; *and he* [who] made him governour over Egypt, and all his houſe." In the two Bibles juſt mentioned, as well as in Tyndal's, and in Coverdale's, και κατεςησεν is properly rendered; and it would have become king James's tranſlators to have followed thoſe Verſions, inſtead of copying after the Biſhops-Bible, which has thrown a miſt over a clear ſentence.

Acts VII. 10.

"Our fathers had the tabernacle of witneſs in the wilderneſs, *as he had appointed, ſpeaking unto Moſes, that he ſhould make it* &c. [as *God* had appointed, when he directed Moſes to make it &c.]" Unleſs it be thus altered, the Pronoun *he*, in the firſt inſtance, muſt refer to the god Remphan, of whom mention was made in the preceding verſe. There is no obſcurity here in the Vulgate: "Sicut diſpoſuit illis *Deus*, loquens ad Moyſen" but Beza has departed from it without reaſon on this, as well as on many other occaſions. Wicklif has followed the Vulgate: "as *God* diſpoſide to hem and ſpak to Moiſes" and ſo has the author of the Spaniſh Verſion: "como les ordenó *Dios*, hablando à Moyſen."

— — 44.

"*And Saul was conſenting unto his death* [Saul conſented unto *Stephen's* death]" Biſhop Barrington very juſtly obſerves, that this clauſe belongs to the preceding chapter; and that it is one among a variety of proofs of the improper diviſion of chapters. We find it

— VIII. 1.

---

* The firſt edition of this Bible was publiſhed, I believe, in 1576. It is crowded with notes tranſlated from Beza, and others, and differs a little from the Geneva Verſion.

it joined to the preceding chapter in the Rhemish translation of the N. T. and in the Version of L'Enfant and Beaufobre.

Acts IX. 27. " But Barnabas took him, and brought him to the Apostles, and declared unto them, how he had seen the Lord in the way, *and that he* [who] had spoken to him, and how he had preached boldly at Damascus in the name of Jesus." This slight alteration, which is requisite in so many places, removes the ambiguity. Thus the Zurich Version: " Barnabas autem acceptum eum duxit ad Apostolos, et narravit eis quomodo in via vidisset Dominum, *qui* locutus est ei &c." There is the same obscurity in the Vulgate, and in Beza, as in our present Version; because they have rendered και ὁτι ελαλησεν αυτω " quia locutus est ei" instead of " *qui* locutus est ei."

—XV. 2. " When therefore Paul and Barnabas had no small dissension and *disputation* [dispute] with them, *they determined* [it was determined] that Paul and Barnabas, *and certain other of them* [with some others] should go up to Jerusalem, &c." According to our Version, the Jewish zealots, who came from Judæa determined, that Paul and Barnabas should lay the matter before the council at Jerusalem; whereas this resolution was taken by the church of Antioch. Εταξαν must either be rendered by what is commonly called an Impersonal, as in the French and Italian Versions; and likewise by Beza, " *constitutum fuit.*" Or, it must be rendered after Schmidius's manner " constituerunt *fratres*" which is adopted by Purver " *the brethren* appointed Paul and Barnabas &c."

—— 5. " But there *rose up certain* [had risen up some] of the sect of the Pharisees, *which believed, saying* [who were Christian converts and said] that it was needful to circumcise *them*, and to command them

them to keep the law of Moses." In the Original, περιτεμνειν αυτους refers to the Gentiles, which is a very remote Antecedent; but that this is contrary to the genius of our language, has been above shewn. It ought therefore to be rendered " that it was *necessary* to circumcise *the Gentiles*" agreeably to which is the Version of Mons: " qu' il falloit circoncire *les Gentils*" and likewise that by L' Enfant and Beausobre: " prétendant que *les Gentils* doivent se faire circoncire" and the same in the Italian: " che convien circoncidere *i Gentili*." The authors of these Versions thought it requisite to name *the Gentiles*, because the Pronoun would not have had otherwise a definite Antecedent.

" *So when they were dismissed* [As soon as they were dismissed] they came to Antioch; and when they had gathered the multitude together, they delivered the epistle: (31) *Which when they* [which after the Gentile converts, or, the converts at Antioch] had read, they rejoyced for *the consolation* [the comfortable tidings."] Αναγνοντες and εχαρησαν must refer to these converts, and not to Paul &c. as the Pronoun *they* intimates. I have seen no translations, in which this verse is rendered properly, except in those by Diodati, and L' Enfant and Beausobre. The former says: " E quando que' d'*Antiochia* l' hebber letta, si rallegrarono della consolazione." The latter: " Eux donc, après avoir été ainsi envoyez, allerent à Antioche, ou ayant assemblé *tous les Fidèles*, ils leur rendirent la lettre, dont la lecture les remplit de joye." Acts XV. 30.

" But Paul thought it not good to take him with *them*, who departed *from* them *from* Pamphylia." This perplexed and ungrammatical sentence may be made tolerably easy and accurate in the following manner: " But Paul thought it not proper to take with them him, who had deserted them in Pamphylia." Or, — — 38.

F we

we may omit "*with them*," which words are in the foregoing verse.

Acts XVI. 1. "*Then he came* [*Paul* came] to Derbe and Lystra: and behold! a certain disciple was there named *Timotheus* [Timothy] (the son of a certain woman *which* [who] was a Jewess, *and believed*; [and a Christian convert;] but his father was a Greek) (2) *which* [who] was well reported of by the *brethren that were* [brethren] at Lystra and Iconium." Bishop Pearce proposes to place υἱος — Ἑλληνος in a parenthesis, which has been adopted by Mr. Bowyer, who has thereby removed the obscurity that was in the printed Greek copies, and in most of the Versions, as well as in ours.

— — 14. "And a certain woman named Lydia, a seller of purple, of the city of Thyatira, *which worshipped God* [and a Jewish proselyte] heard us; *whose heart the Lord opened that* [and the Lord opened her heart so that] she attended to the things which were spoken *of* [by] Paul." The Version of Mons is not in the least ambiguous: "elle nous écouta; et le Seigneur luy ouvrit le cœur pour entendre avec soumission ce qui Paul disoit" Nor is the Italian: "stava ad ascoltare; e l'Signore aperse il suo cuore &c." Nor is the Spanish: "temerosa de Dios oyó; el coraçon de la qual abrió el Señor &c." Had our Translators rendered "ηκουσεν" differently, they would have kept clear of any ambiguity; but by injudiciously adding "*us*" as a supplemental reading, they have asserted, that the Lord opened the heart, not of Lydia, but of Paul and his companions.

— XVII. 1. "*Now when they had passed* [*After Paul and Silas* had passed] through Amphipolis, they came to Thessalonica, where was a synagogue of the Jews."

— — 5. "*But the Jews which believed not* [But the unbelieving Jews] moved

moved with envy, *took unto them certain lewd fellows* [took some wicked fellows] of the baser sort, and gathered a company, and set all the city *on* [in] an uproar, and assaulted the house of Jason *and sought to bring them out* [and sought after *Paul and Silas*, that they might bring them out] to the people." It is necessary to mention by name Paul and Silas, because otherwise the Antecedent to "*them*," is either " the devout Greeks " or " the chief women." The French Versions alone seem to be perfectly clear as to this point. Thus that of Mons: " voulant enlever *Paul & Silas*, & les mener devant tout le peuple," and so that of L'Enfant and Beausobre: " Cherchant *Paul & Silas*." I have rendered, with the Geneva Bible printed by Barker 1576, πονηρες ανδρας, " wicked " not " lewd " men; for whatever meaning the latter epithet might bear at the time that our present Version was made, it certainly cannot now be applied to the men of whom St. Luke speaks. But it is observable, that Wicklif renders it "*summe yvele men*" in which he has been followed by almost all the translators even to the reign of James I.—— It will not be amiss to correct a similar expression in Acts XVIII. 14. " And when Paul was *now about to open his mouth* [preparing to speak] Gallio said unto the Jews, If it were a matter of wrong, *or wicked lewdness* [or evil propensity] O ye Jews, *reason would that I should bear with you*, [it would be but reasonable, that I should hear you patiently."] ραδιουργημα, which is derived from two words, cannot, I think, be expressed by any one word better than by *propensity*. In our old Bibles ραδιουργημα πονηρον is rendered " an evel deed " not " wicked lewdness." Let the reader judge, whether our Translators have improved their Version by departing from this interpretation.

" And

Acts XVII. 8.   "And they troubled the people, and the rulers of the city, when *they heard* these things." It seems uncertain, whether the words "they heard" refer to the Christian converts, or to the rulers of the city; but a very small change in the construction of the sentence will make it clear: "And the people, and the rulers of the city were greatly disturbed, when they heard these things." Thus Tremellius: "Turbati autem sunt principes civitatis et universus populus, quum audivissent hæc."

—XVIII. 7.   "And he departed thence, and entered into *a certain man's house named Justus*, [the house of a certain man, named Justus] *one that worshipped God, whose house joined hard* [a Jewish proselyte whose house was very near] to the synagogue." Of all the translators Castalio hath avoided the most carefully any incorrectness, as to the Relative and Antecedent: "Ita illinc profectus, venit in ædes cujusdam nomine Justi, hominis religiosi, cujus ædes erant contiguæ collegio." But "religiosi" does not at all point out the true meaning of σεβομενε τον Θεον, nor was it proper to render συναγωγη by "collegio," for which he has been justly animadverted upon by many writers; though at the same time it must be acknowledged, that there are some places in the N. T. where it ought not to be translated "synagogue."

—XXI. 20.   "And when they heard it, they glorified the Lord, *and said unto him*, Thou seest, brother, how many thousands of the Jews there are *which* [who] believe." It had better be rendered "and said *unto Paul*" for though it is not probable, that the sense of this passage should be misunderstood, yet, as it has been said above, it is the business of a translator to guard against the possibility of a doubt. Upon this principle Castalio has inserted the regular Antecedent: "Quibus auditis illi, actis Domino gratiis, Paullum

sic

fic alloquuntur" and likewife Diodati: "Ed effi uditele, glorificavano Iddio: poi differo à *Paolo*" and alfo L'Enfant and Beaufobre: " Mais ils dirent a *Paul* &c."

" On the morrow they left the horfemen to go with him, and returned to the caftle: (33) *Who* when they came to Cæfarea &c." The Relative *who* muft neceffarily refer here to the foldiers that *returned*; whereas it ought to be connected with the horfemen. There is the fame fault in the Vulgate which has been avoided by Beza: " Poftero autem die, reverfi funt in caftra, relictis equitibus qui cum eo proficifcerentur: Qui cum veniffent Cæfaream &c." We may tranfpofe the words in the fame manner: " Upon the next day, they returned to the caftle, and left the horfemen to go with him; (33) Who after their arrival at Cæfarea, delivered the epiftle &c." So the Verfion of Mons: " Et de lendemain ils s'en retournerent à la fortereffe l' ayant laiffé entre les mains des Cavaliers; qui eftant arrivez à Cæfareé &c." The fenfe is very clear in Diodati: E'l giorno fequente, lafciati i cavalieri per andar con lui, ritornarono alla Rocca; E *quelli*, giunti in Cefarea, &c."

Acts XXIII. 32.

" And after five days, Ananias the high prieft *defcended* with the elders, and with a certain orator named Tertullus, *who* informed the governour againft Paul." In this verfe the Relative *who* feems to Tertullus only as its Antecedent; whereas in the Original ἰτινες certainly includes Ananias, and the elders, and Tertullus alfo. Here our language appears to be defective. Perhaps the ambiguity might be removed by rendering the paffage thus: " After five days, Ananias the high prieft *went down* with the elders, and with a certain orator named Tertullus, and laid before the

— XXIV. 1.

the governour *their* informations againſt Paul." The Spaniſh, Italian, and French Verſions are not in the leaſt equivocal upon this head. Thus the Spaniſh Verſion: " Y cinco dias deſpues deſcendió el Principe de los Sacerdotes, Ananias, con los Ancianos, y Tertullo un Orador: y *parecieron* delante del Preſidente contra Pablo." Thus Diodati: " Hor, cinque giorni appreſſo, il ſommo Sacerdote Anania diſceſe, inſieme con gli Antiani, e con un certo Tertullo oratore: e *comparvero* davanti al Governatore contr' a Paolo." So the Verſion of Mons: " Cinque jours après Ananie grand Preſtre deſcendit à Ceſareé avec quelques Senateurs et un certain orateur nommé Tertulle, *qui ſe rendirent* accuſateurs de Paul devant le Gouverneur."

Acts XXVIII. 1.

" *And when they were eſcaped* [After *Paul and the mariners* had eſcaped] then they knew that the iſland was called Melita." Stephens has put οἱ περι τον Παυλον εκ τȣ πλοες in his margin after διασωθεντες, and has cited two MSS. for it; but even independently of them we ought to inſert the proper Antecedent at the beginning of the chapter. The Vulgate has rendered it: " Et cum evaſiſſemus, tunc cognovimus" and this is ſupported by the Alexandrian MS. in which we find επεγνωμεν: a reading, which is approved of by Bengelius; and which the author of the Spaniſh Verſion has adopted: " Y como *eſcapamos,* entonces *conoſcimos* la iſla, que ſe llamava Melita." The ſame is in the Verſion of Mons: " *Nous* étant ainſi ſauvez, *nous* reconnuſmes &c." Thus likewiſe Wicklif: " And whanne we hadde aſcaped, thanne we knewen &c." and Coverdale: " And whan we were eſcaped, we knew that the iſle was called Melyte." I ſhould prefer this reading, on account of the verſe immediately following, Οἱ δε βαρβαροι παρειχον παρειχεν ου την τυχουσαν φιλανθρωπιαν ημιν &c." It is rather to be wondered at, that Beza should write a long note upon the first verse, without taking any notice of the different reading abovementioned.

CHAPTER IV.

Ambiguities occasioned by equivocal Words or Phrases.

"THEREFORE is the kingdom of heaven *likened* [like] unto a certain king *which would take account of his servants* [who resolved to settle his accounts with his servants."] According to our present Version, he seemed to have no other view, than to compute the number of his servants. It is not so in Wicklif: " Therfore the kyngdom of hevens is likned to a kyng that wolde *rikene* with his servantis." Nor in Coverdale: " which wolde *reken* with his servauntes."

Matth. XVIII. 23.

" The servant therefore fell down, and *worshipped him* [humbly entreated him."] Mintert furnishes us with many instances of this signification of the Verb προσκυνεω in the LXX, and my learned friend Mr. Harmer has put the meaning of this, and of similar passages, beyond all doubt, in his description of the various methods of doing persons honour in the Holy-Land*. It is very properly rendered by Wicklif " But thilke servaunt fell down and

— — 26.

---

* Observations on divers passages of Scripture, vol. II. ch. vi.

and *preide* him" and by the authors of the Geneva Version " besought him" which king James's translators chose rather to insert
in their margin, than in their text. Had they in other chapters
been more sparing in the use of the word "worship" which they
must have known to be equivocal, they would have represented
more clearly the sense of the Original. One of the strangest examples in this kind is in Luke XIV. 10. " But when thou art
bidden, [invited] go and sit down in the lowest *room* [seat] that
when he *that bade thee* [who invited thee] cometh, he may say
unto thee, Friend, go up higher: then shalt thou have *worship*
[honour, or, respect] in the presence of them, *that sit at meat*
[who sit at table] with thee." Bishop Pearce observes, that in
this antient sense of the word *worship*, which is, respect or reverence, our form of matrimony says " with my body I thee worship" but were these expressions a little new-modelled, it could
give no reasonable offence.

Matt. XX. 26.

" But it shall not be so among you; *but whosoever will be* [*for*
whosoever desires to be] great among you let him *be your minister*
[assist you, or, attend upon you.] Διακονος imports no more than
this; and is translated after this manner in the Spanish and
French Versions. If it be rendered by "minister" as, in fact, it
is in almost all our Bibles, except in the later editions of the
Geneva Version, it cannot but lead the common people to imagine, that it denotes a person in Holy Orders. So again Acts
XIII. 5. " And when they were at Salamis, they preached the
word of God in the synagogue of the Jews; *and they had also John
to their minister*" It should be " and had also John *for* their assist-
ant, or attendant." Thus L'Enfant and Beausobre " ils avoient
Jean avec eux *pour leur aider*" There are indeed many passages
which

which require correction, where "miniſtering" ſhould be rendered by "waiting upon" or "ſupplying with food, or with alms." We read in Acts VI. 1. "there aroſe a murmuring of the Græcians againſt the Hebrews, becauſe their widows were neglected *in the daily miniſtration.*" It ought to be "in the daily diſtribution of alms."

"Therefore *ſay I* [I ſay] unto you, the kingdom of God ſhall be taken from you, and given *to a nation bringing forth* [to the Gentiles who will bring forth] the fruits thereof." There is no doubt, that the primitive Chriſtians knew, that εθνει comprehended the whole body of the Gentiles; but an unlettered Engliſhman will naturally conſider the word in our Verſion as applied to a particular people. Tyndal has properly rendered it "to the Gentyles" and Coverdale "unto the Heythen." Matt. XXI. 43.

"For he knew *that for envy they had delivered him* [that out of malice they had delivered him *up.*"] It is worthy of obſervation, that our Tranſlators have uſed the expreſſion *delivered up* in Acts III. 13. though they have omitted it in numberleſs other places, where the ſame mode of expreſſion was equally required. —XXVII. 18.

"But the chief prieſts and elders perſuaded the people, *that they ſhould aſk Barabbas*, and deſtroy Jeſus." It ſhould be "to aſk *for* Barabbas" or rather "*for the releaſe of* Barabbas." To aſk Barabbas, has a very different meaning.—So Mark IV. 10. "And when he was *alone* [in private] they who were about him with the twelve, aſked of him *the parable* [the meaning, or interpretation of the parable] I have rendered Ὅτι δε εγενετο καταμονας "When he was in private" becauſe it cannot be ſaid with any propriety, that he was *alone.* Thus L'Enfant and Beauſobre: "Lorſqu'il fut en particulier." —XX.

G

"For

Mar. III. 10. "*For he had healed* many, infomuch that they preffed upon him *for* to touch him, as many as had *plagues*." It would be better thus: "For he was healing many, infomuch that as many as had *grievous diftempers*, preffed upon him to touch him." The word *plague* might poffibly mean any kind of a fevere difeafe in the laft century; but it is now appropriated to a particular one. The fame alteration fhould take place in fimilar paffages. It is obfervable, that Wicklif does not render μαςιγας "plagues" but "ficknefſis."

——IV. 33. "And with many fuch parables *fpake he* [he fpake] the word unto them, *as they were able to hear it*." The latter part of the verfe is fo expreffed, as to fuggeft a meaning very different from the Original. It would be better "according as they were capable of underftanding it." Thus Schmidius: "prout poterant intellectu affequi" and L'Enfant and Beaufobre: "felon leur porteé."

Luke VII. 16. "And there came a fear on all; and they glorified God, faying, that a great prophet is rifen up among us; and that God hath *vifited his people*, [taken care, or, the charge of his people.]" This is implied by the Verb επισκεψατο, and feems much more proper than *vifited*, which in Scripture often bears an oppofite meaning; and it would not be amifs to alter our Verfion in other places. I would render with Mr. Wakefield επισκεψασθε με "ye took care of me" in Matth. XXV. 36.

——XI. 39. "And the Lord faid unto him, *Now do ye Pharifees make clean the outfide of the cup and the platter &c.*" It would be better "Now ye Pharifees make clean" or rather "Now ye Pharifees do make clean" for it is a declaration of our Saviour, and ought not to have the appearance of an Interrogative Sentence. It is obvioufly an Explicative Sentence in Wicklif's tranflation: "And the

the Lord feide unto him, now ye Farifees clenfen" and likewife in the Geneva Bible: " And the Lord faid to him, In dede ye Pharifes make cleane &c." I cannot help remarking, that there are feveral paffages in our prefent Verfion, where a queftion feems to be afked, when, in fact, a thing is commanded to be done.

" And the younger of them faid to his father, Father, give me the portion of goods that *falleth* [is to fall] to me. And he divided *unto them his living* [between them his fubftance."] Βιος ought to be rendered fo in other paffages, and not by a word of a doubtful fignification; and I cannot but wonder, that our Tranflators neglected to follow the old Verfions, in which it is rendered by " fubftance." Luke XV. 12.

" And when he was *demanded of* [afked by] the Pharifees, when the kingdom of God fhould come, *he anfwered them, and faid* [he anfwered] the kingdom of God cometh not *with obfervation*." To be *demanded of* the Pharifees, and to be *afked by* them, have now two very different meanings. In a marginal note in our prefent Verfion, μετα παρατηρησεως is rendered by " outward fhew;" but why fhould it not be " the kingdom of God *will* not come fo as to be obferved." This is more literal than the note, as well as more eafy than the text. ——XVII. 20.

" *And it came to pafs that on one of thofe days as he taught* [While *Jefus* upon one of thofe days was teaching] the people in the temple, and *preached* [preaching] the gofpel, the chief priefts and the fcribes *came upon him, with the elders*." Admirable indeed! as if they intended to deftroy the elders, as well as Jefus. We muft invert the order of the words thus: " the chief priefts, and the fcribes, with the elders came upon him." It is right in Tyndal: " the hie prieftes and the fcribes came wyth the elders, and fpake unto ——XX. 1.

unto him faying" and likewife in Wicklif: "And it was don in oon of the dayes, whanne he taughte the peple in the temple, and prechide the gofpel: the princis of preftis and fcribis camen togidre with the eldre men."—— The like inaccuracy occurs in Acts XXI. 5. "And they all brought us on our way, *with wives and children.*" This is copied literally from Cranmer's, and the Bifhops-Bible. Have we any other intimation of St. Paul and St. Luke travelling with wives and children? It probably would be in vain to look any where elfe for this curious circumftance. We fhould either render it "And they all, with *their* wives and children, brought us on our way" or "and they all brought us on our way, with *their* wives and children" as it is rendered by Tyndal, Mathew, and Taverner. But it cannot be tranflated better than in Tomfon's, and in the Geneva Bible: "And they all accompanied us, with *their* wives and children."

Luke XXIII. 11. "And Herod with his *men of war fet him at nought* [foldiers, or guards treated him contemptuoufly."]

John I. 21. "And they afked him, What then? Art thou Elias? and he faith, I am not. *Art thou that prophet?* And he anfwered, No." This feems to be a repetition of the fame queftion refpecting Elias. To make it intelligible, we muft either render it by the parallel paffage in St. Luke, as Dr. Lightfoot has done, "Art thou one of the prophets raifed from the dead?" Or "Art thou that prophet promifed to the people of God?" Or "Art thou *the* prophet?" Or "Art thou *a* prophet?" This laft reading is put in the margin of our prefent Verfion, conformably to the Vulgate: "Propheta es tu?" which is adopted by Caftalio, Wicklif, and Tyndal. Beza contends, that fome particular prophet muft necef- farily be alluded to, becaufe the Article ὁ is found in every MS.

but

but it would be very easy to shew, if it were requisite, that there are several passages in the N. T. which ought to be rendered by the Indefinite Article, though the Article ὁ is in the Original.

"Art thou a *master of Israel*, and knowest not these things?" John III. 10. Though the words *master* and *teacher* are often synonimous, yet something very different is implied by a *master of Israel*. It should be rendered "Art thou a *teacher in* Israel?" Not "*of* Israel" as in the Geneva Bible, and as it seems to be recommended by Bishop Pearce; though even this is much better than what is in our present Version.

"Then those men, when they had seen the miracle that Jesus ⸺ VI. 14. did [had done] said, This is *of a truth* [truly] that prophet *that should come into the world* [who was to come, or, who was expected to come into the world.] To say, *that he should come*, is ambiguous; for it may mean, that he *ought* to come. It is "qui venturus erat in mundum" as the Zurich Version says.

"He spake of Judas Iscariot the son of Simon; *for he it was* ⸺ 71. *that should betray him* [for it was he, who was about, or, going to betray him]" futurum enim erat, ut hic proderet eum, as it is in the Zurich Version; and as it is in Wicklif "for this was to bitraie him." A similar correction must be made in ch. XII. 4. How much better does the Vulgate render ὁ μελλων παραδιδοναι by the Participle *traditurus?* The indiscriminate use of *should, would,* and *could*, which is taken notice of by Bishop Lowth, has introduced strange confusion into our Vulgar Translation. I will mention another instance in Acts XXIII. 27. which is part of a letter from Lysias to Felix. "This man was taken *of* [by] the Jews, and *should have been killed by them: then came I with an army* [and *would* have been killed by them; but I suddenly came with a band of *foldiers*] and refcued him, having underftood that he was a Roman." According to our prefent Verfion, Lyfias informs Felix, that he refcued a man, who had deferved death; and, what is not a little extraordinary, he employed nothing lefs than *an army* in taking him out of the hands of the Jews. King James's tranflators followed the Vulgate, in which επι τῳ ϛρατευματι is rendered, *cum exercitu*; but it is much better in Beza " cum militum manu " and in almoft all our old Verfions, which have "*foldiers*." I will fubjoin the tranflation by Coverdale, which needs not fear to be compared with our prefent Verfion: " The Jews had taken thys man, and *wolde* have flayne hym. Then came I with *fouldyers*, and refcued hym."

John XX. 31.
" But thefe are written, that ye *might* [may] believe, *and that believing ye might have life through his name*." Inftead of the Participle *believing*, which makes the fentence appear rather ambiguous, it would be better to fubftitute " and that *by means of* your belief ye *may* have life through his name." It is very clear in Coverdale: " But thefe are written, that ye fhoulde belefe that Jefus is Chrifte the fonne of God, and that ye *therow belefe* might have lyfe in his name."——So Matth. XXI. 22. " *And all things whatfoever* [And whatfoever] ye fhall afk in prayer, *believing, ye fhall receive*." It would be better " if ye have faith, ye fhall receive," or, " ye fhall receive, if ye believe." Here is not the leaft fhadow of ambiguity; nor is there in Coverdale: " And whatfoever ye axe in prayer, if ye belefe, ye fhall receve it."

Acts I. 6.
" *When they therefore* [Therefore as foon as] they were come together, they *afked of him* [afked him] faying, Lord, wilt thou at this time *reftore again* [reftore] the kingdom of Ifrael?" The Apoftles did not allude to any *prior* reftoration. We find it rightly

rightly translated in the Rhemish N. T. and in Tomson's, and in the Geneva Bible.

"For it is written in the book of Psalms, Let his habitation be desolate, and let no man dwell therein; and his *bishoprick* [office] let another take." It is curious enough to represent bishopricks as subsisting under the Mosaic dispensation. But this mode of translating, strange as it is, has been adopted in several Versions; but not by Castalio: "ejusque munus excipiat alius" nor by Diodati: "Un' altro prenda il suo ufficio" nor by L'Enfant and Beausobre: "Qu'un autre soit mis en possession de sa charge" nor by the authors of the English Versions last cited "Let another take his charge." King James's translators ought at least to have turned their attention towards the 109th Psalm, where it is rendered both in the old and new Version "and let another take his office." Purver has rendered την επισκοπην αυτε λαβοι ετερος "let another take his office of *Overseer*" as if he were determined to depart as far as possible from King James's translators; and to intimate to the common people, that Judas Iscariot had been a guardian of the poor; for the word "*Overseer*" how literal soever a translation it may be of επισκοπος, cannot be considered by them in any other light.

Acts I. 20.

"Who received the *lively* oracles to give unto us." Wetstein mentions λογον as being in the editions of Erasmus, Colinæus &c. and this was the reading adopted by the Vulgate, which seems to be unexceptionable. Thus Wicklif: "the wordis of lyf" and to the same purport in Tyndal, Coverdale, and the Bishops-Bible. But if we retain the common reading, viz. λογια ζωντα, we must at least render it "the living oracles," and expunge the equivocal epithet "lively."

—. VII. 38.

"But

Acts XI. 4. "But Peter *rehearsed the matter* [related the transaction] from the beginning, and *expounded it by order* unto them." Either, "regularly expounded it" or "expounded it *in* order" as in most of our old Versions; for "by order" implies, that he was commanded to do it.

— XII. 11. "And when Peter was come to himself, he said, Now *I know of a surety* [certainly, or truly know] that the Lord hath sent his angel &c." The expression in our Version is ambiguous, and therefore ought to be avoided. It is so indeed in Cranmer's, and the Bishops-Bible; but far different in Tomson's, and in the Geneva Versions, in which it is rendered: "Now I know for a trueth."

— XIII. 2. "*As they ministered to the Lord and fasted* [While they were ministering to the Lord, and fasting] the Holy Ghost said, Separate *me* [FOR me] Barnabas and Saul for the work *whereunto* [to which] I have called them." Most of the English translators, by omitting the Preposition, have unwarily given a very odd turn to this passage. Bishop Lowth says, "that the Prepositions *to* and *for* are often understood; as "give me the book; get me some paper;" that is, *to* me, *for* me *." It is undoubtedly true in these, and similar phrases, where the sense can hardly be misapprehended; but can any one think, that the Preposition *for* is necessarily understood in this sentence "Separate me Paul and Barnabas." It evidently must appear to mean "Separate us all three." His Lordship should have pointed out some exceptions to which this mode of writing is liable.

— — 15. "And after the reading of the law and the prophets, the rulers of the synagogue sent to them, saying, *Ye men and brethren*, [Brethren]

---

* Introduction to English grammar p. 145.

thren] if ye have any word of exhortation to the people, *say on.*" This expreffion intimates, as Bifhop Pearce has obferved, that Paul and Barnabas had fpoken before; whereas the reverfe of it is true. It is well known, and remarked by many commentators, that it was ufual for the rulers of the fynagogues to afk ftrangers, after fome parts of Scripture had been expounded, if they wifhed to communicate any inftruction to the people. Accordingly, they addreffed Paul and Barnabas to this purpofe: λεγετε " fpeak," that is, You may *now* fpeak, if you pleafe. It is rendered properly in the Rhemifh N. T. " fpeake," and by Wicklif " fcie ghe."

" And when they had *ordained them elders* [appointed elders *over* them] in every church, and had prayed *with fafting,* [and fafted] they commended them unto the Lord &c." The omiffion of the Prepofition in our Verfion intirely alters the fenfe, as in ch. XXIII. 2. How much better is the rendering by Wicklif! " And whanne thei hadden ordeyned preftis *to* hem &c."   Acts XIV. 23.

" God *that made* [who made] the world and all things therein, *feeing that he is* [being] Lord of heaven and earth, dwelleth not in temples made with hands." 'Υπαρχων ought here to be rendered by " being." *Seeing that* was commonly ufed in the laft century for *fince*; but it is now obfolete: and indeed, from its ambiguity, was very improperly admitted into this verfe. The like occurs in that which immediately follows. " Neither is worfhipped with men's hands, *as though* [as if] he needeth any thing; *feeing* [fince] he giveth to *all* [every one] life, and breath, and all things."   XVII. 24.

" For a certain man named Demetrius, a filverfmith, *which* [who] made filver fhrines *for* [of] Diana," or rather " made filver models *of* Diana's temple &c." Did our Tranflators imagine, that Demetrius was employed by Diana herfelf? Nothing can be clearer   XIX. 24.

clearer than the Original, ποιων ναους αργυρους Αρτεμιδος, which is faithfully rendered in Tomson's, and in the Geneva Bible "made silver temples *of* Diana."

Acts XXI. 15.

" And after three days *we took up carriages and* [we being prepared for the journey] went up to Jerusalem." Thus Mr. Markland translates επισκευασαμενοι, which is the reading that he prefers; and he very justly doubts, whether St. Paul and his companions (if we except the Cæsareans) had any other carriages than their own shoulders; and perhaps a stick or pole upon which each carried his own bundle. The true sense is preserved in the Bishops-Bible, though rather vulgarly expressed " we toke up our burthens;" but the terms are still more coarse in the Geneva Bible: " we trussed up our fardels." It is very well in Wicklif: " we weren maad redi." And in Coverdale: " we were ready."

— — 25.

" *As touching the Gentiles which believe* [In respect to the Gentile converts] we have written, *and concluded that they observe no such thing* [and *determined* that they *shall* observe no such thing &c."] I have taken the word " determined" from the Geneva Bible. " To conclude that they observe no such thing" is totally foreign to the subject.

— — XXIV. 12.

" And they neither found me in the temple disputing with any man, *neither raising up the people* [nor stirring up the people], *neither* [either] in the synagogues, *nor* [or] in the city." It is exceedingly strange, that so many translators should have used the expression " raising up," which ought to be consecrated to another purpose. They had much better have rendered επισυστασιν ποιουντα οχλου " making an uproar among the people," as in Coverdale, and in the Geneva Bible; or, as in Wicklif " making concours of peple."

" Let

"Let them therefore, said he, *which* among you are *able*, go down with me, and accuse this man, if there be any *wickedness* in him." Can any word have a more indeterminate meaning than "able" in this verse? There are various interpretations of δυνατοι: but most probably it denotes such as could give the best information; in which sense we find it used by the LXX in II. Chron. XXXV. 3. as cited by Mintert. I should therefore translate the verse thus: "Let such therefore, he said, as *can give the best information*, go down with me, and accuse this man, if there be *any thing amiss* in him." In rendering the last line, I have followed Bishop Pearce and Dr. Owen, who say, that ατοπον is in many MSS.

Acts XXV. 5.

CHAPTER V.

Ambiguities occasioned by an indeterminate Use of Prepositions.

IT is observed by Bishop Lowth, that the Preposition *of* is much the same with *from*; "ask *of* me," that is, *from* me: "made *of* wood;" "Son *of* Philip;" that is, sprung *from* him*. There is no doubt, that it may be used after this manner; and likewise for the Preposition *by*; but particular care should be taken, that the sense of a passage be presented to us without the least possibility of a mistake; the contrary of which is sometimes found in

* Introduction to English grammar, p. 97.

our Vulgar translation; and which was not unworthy of his Lordship's notice.

Matth. I. 18.   " Now the birth of Jesus Christ was *on this wise: when as his mother Mary was espoused to Joseph* [after this manner: his mother Mary being contracted to Joseph] before they came together, she was found with child *of* [by] the Holy Ghost."

—— — 20.   " Fear not to take unto thee Mary thy wife; for that which is conceived in her is *of* [by] the Holy Ghost." It is observable, that some of our early translators use the Preposition *by* in ver. 18. and *of* in ver. 20. but the Rhemish N. T. is right in both in-instances, as our present Version is evidently wrong.

—XIX. 12.   " And there are some eunuchs *which* [who] were made eunuchs *of men* [by men.]

Luke VI. 45.   " For *of* [from] the abundance of the heart his mouth speaketh."

——IX. 7.   " Now Herod the tetrarch heard of all that *was done* [had been done] by him; *and he was* [and was] perplexed, *because that* [because] it was said *of* [by] some that John was risen from the dead: (8) and *of* [by] some, that Elias had appeared; and *of* [by] others, that one of the old prophets was risen again."

——XXII. 71.   " And they said, What need *we* [have we of] any further witness? for we ourselves have heard *of* [enough from, or, it from] his own mouth?"

John VIII. 26.   " I have many things to say, and *to judge of you,* [to condemn in you] but he *that* [who] sent me is true; and I speak to the world those things, which I have heard *of* [from] him."

—— — 40.   " But now ye seek to kill me, a man *that* [who] hath told you the truth, which I have heard *of* [from] God &c."

——XV. 15.   " But I have called you friends; for all things that I have heard *of* [from] my Father, I have made known unto you."

" And

"And one Ananias, a devout man according to the law, having a good report *of all the Jews which* [among all the Jews who] dwelt there." — Acts XXII. 12.

"And when there arose a great diffension, the chief captain fearing left Paul should have been pulled in pieces *of them* [by them] commanded the foldiers to go down &c." — XXIII. 10.

It is evident, that in these instances the Preposition *of* is very improperly used; for in some it seems to bear the same signification as the Preposition *concerning*; and in others to denote the Genitive Case; so that in all it introduces a new meaning widely different from the Original.

The following examples likewise shew, that the Preposition *with* is sometimes injudiciously used for *by* and *through*.

"But in every nation he *that* [who] feareth him, and worketh righteousness, is accepted *with him* [by him.]" To say "that one person shall be accepted *with* another" is much the same as to say "that they shall both be accepted." Of all our antient Versions, the Rhemish N. T. is the most accurate in this instance, in which it is rendered "acceptable to him." — X. 35.

"And when they were come to Jerusalem, they were *received of the church* [received with approbation by the church] and *of* [by] the Apostles and elders; and they declared all things *that God had done with them*." It ought to be "that God had done *through* them," that is, through their ministry. We see in Mintert, that when μετα has a Genitive Case after it, it is used by the LXX to signify *per*, as well as cum &c. Beza has rightly translated it "quanta Deus *per* ipsos effeciffet." It is rendered by Tyndal, and by the authors of the Geneva Version "that God had done *by* them," but this is as liable to exception, as *with them;* — XV. 4.

them; for both phrafes are ambiguous. In the tranflation of ἀπεδέχθησαν I have followed Mr. Pyle, who has given this Verb its full and due force; and to whom we are much indebted for his ufeful paraphrafe and notes on the Acts of the Apoftles, and the Epiftles.——The fame obfervation, which has been here made, is applicable to XIV. 27. "And when they were come, and gathered the people together, *they rehearfed all that God had done with them.*" It fhould be "they *related* all that God had done *through* them."

CHAPTER VI.

Upon Paffages ungrammatical.

HAVING confidered fome of the ambiguities in our prefent Verfion, we are in the next place to inquire, whether the language be conformable to the rules of Grammar. This method would be obferved in examining the tranflation of a Claffical compofition; and no good reafon can be affigned, why it fhould not be adopted in examining that of the Bible: efpecially fince it is my defign, in this effay, to confine my remarks to language alone.

It might naturally be expected, that, in a preface of fo formidable a length, our Tranflators would have explained the principles by which they were guided in forming their ftyle; but, inftead of this, they do little more than awkardly defend their neglect

lect of rendering uniformly. They amuse themselves and their readers with putting the following question: " Is the kingdom of God become words or syllables?" The answer is obvious. Though we ought always to pay a stricter attention to things than to words, yet it must be invariably allowed, that we cannot convey an adequate idea of the former, without fully comprehending the propriety of the latter. But our Translators, not content with offering their sentiments in this brisk manner, take occasion to advance a general maxim " that a niceness of words was always counted the next step to trifling." Surely it became persons invested with so important a trust, to have spoken with more caution and reserve on this head. They ought either not to have used such loose and unguarded terms; or not to have left to their readers the necessity of exploring the drift of them. If they mean only, that a laboured or florid style is inconsistent with the simplicity of the Gospel, their opinion would be universally admitted; but if their design is to insinuate, what does not seem wholly improbable, that grammatical accuracy was beneath their consideration, they can scarcely appear to have deserved the eulogies, which have been so lavishly bestowed upon them. I should be sorry to be thought to speak of them too harshly; or to ascribe to them any sentiments which they did not entertain; but the general tenor of their Version of the four Gospels, and of the Acts of the Apostles, must induce us to conclude, that they had not a thorough knowledge of Grammar and Syntax; or, at least, that they did not sufficiently attend to the rules of them. As the instances in this kind are exceedingly numerous, I shall select only a few specimens; and, for the sake of method, shall dispose them under six different heads.

I. *In*

(64)

I. *In respect to Participles, and the Modes and Times of Verbs.*

Matth. V. 23.
"Therefore, if thou bring thy gift to the altar, and there *remembrest* that thy brother hath *aught* [any *matter of complaint* against thee &c."] It should be "remember" for the Hypothetical Conjunction *if*, as used in this verse, must necessarily suppose something contingent; and of course require the Subjunctive Mode after it. Besides, as Bishop Lowth has observed, nothing can be more improper, than for the same Conjunction to govern both the Subjunctive and Indicative Mode, in the same sentence, and in the same circumstances*. Not one of our old Versions has translated correctly this verse in St. Matthew. Thus Wicklif: "Therefore if thou offrist thi gifte at the auter, and there thou bithenkist &c." Here is indeed no confusion of Modes, as in our present Version; but the Subjunctive ought to have been used, because something doubtful was implied. Tyndal, with many others, renders it: "Therefore *when* thou offerest thy gyft at the altare, and there remembrest &c." That the Conjunction εαν sometimes ought to be translated *when*, appears from the passages cited by Mr. Parkhurst out of the N. T. but the Hypothetical Conjunction *if* is more proper in this verse.

—XXVI. 67.
"Then did they *spit in* his face, and *buffeted* him." Either it should be "Then did they spit *on* his face, and buffet him," or "Then they *spat on* his face, and buffeted him," the last of which is in the Geneva Bible.

—XXVII. 30.
"And they *spit* upon him, and took the reed &c." Here it cer-

---

* Introduction to English grammar, p. 156.

certainly ought to be "spat," because "took" is a Verb of Past Time. It is rendered by Tyndal, and Coverdale, and by the authors of the Geneva Bible, " And they *spitted* upon him, and took &c." which is more accurate than what is in our Version, though perhaps not perfectly right.

"And *at even* [in the evening] when the sun *did set* &c. [was set &c."] There is the same impropriety in Tomson's Bible: " and when even was come, at what time the sun *setteth*;" for the Verb *set* is an Active Verb, and therefore improperly made Neuter. It is well rendered in most of the old Versions " when the sun was *down*." In Coverdale: " when the sunne was *gone down*."   Mark I. 32.

"And he cometh to Bethsaida, and they bring a blind man unto him, and *besought* him to touch him." It ought to be " beseech." The three Verbs *come*, *bring*, and *beseech*, are in Present Time in the Original; so that king James's translators cannot be justified for writing incorrect English, upon the plea of rendering literally. Mr. Wynne and Mr. Purver have followed these translators instead of the old Versions, in which it is uniformly well rendered " came " " brought " and " desired " all in the same Time.   ——VIII. 22.

"And he took the blind man by the hand, and led him out of the town, and when he had *spit* on his eyes, and put his hand upon him, he asked him, if he saw *aught* [any thing."] It should be *spitten*, for this is the true Participle, as *sitten* is of the Verb *to sit*. Mr. Purver, in his fanciful catalogue of *words ill joined together*, has corrected Luke XVIII. 32. " shall be spitted on," pretending, that it ought to be " shall be spit on;" but both expressions are equally wrong.

I   " And

John V. 16.   "And therefore *did* the Jews *perfecute* Jefus, and *fought* to flay him, becaufe he had done thefe things on the fabbath-day." It ought either to be "did perfecute and feek," or "perfecuted and fought."

——XIX. 24.   "They faid therefore among themfelves, Let us not *rent* it &c." Either "rend it," or "divide it," as in Tyndal, and in moft of our old Verfions.—There is a worfe fault in Matth. XXVII. 51. "And behold! the veil of the temple was rent *in twain* [in two, or, in pieces] from the top to the bottom; and the earth *did quake* [trembled] and the rocks *rent* [were rent.]" There are undoubtedly fome Englifh Verbs which have both an Active and a Neuter fignification; but the Verb "to rend" is not of this clafs; yet even if it were, it would be improperly ufed in its two Forms, in the fame fentence; for this, how agreeable foever to the learned languages, feems contrary to the genius of our own.

——XX. 5.   "And he ftooping down, and looking in, faw the linen-clothes *lying*: yet went he not in: (6) Then cometh Simon Peter following him, and *went* [goeth] into the fepulchre, and feeth the linen-clothes *lie*; (7) And the napkin *that was* [which had been] about his head, not *lying* with the linen-clothes, but wrapped together in a place by itfelf." To ufe here both the Infinitive Mode "to lie" and the Participle "lying" is very incorrect; yet it is fo in all the old Verfions which I have examined, except in the Rhemifh N. T. where the Participle "lying" is uniformly ufed. Nothing is more frequent both in common converfation, and in writing, than to ufe a Verb, immediately following another, in the Infinitive Mode, without the Prepofition or fign *to*; of which Bifhop Lowth has given fome inftances [*]; but I cannot help think-

---

[*] Introduction to Englifh grammar, p. 117.

thinking, that, in one or two of them the Participle is more proper, than the Infinitive Mode.

"But Peter continued knocking: and when they had opened the door, and *saw* him, they were astonished." It either should be "seen" the Participle in the Past Time, or it should be rendered "*they* saw him, *and* were astonished." Thus Wicklif: "and whanne thei hadden opened the dore, they saighen him, and wondriden;" and in the same manner Coverdale: "Whan they opened the dore, they sawe him, and were astonyed." It is strange, that king James's translators did not choose rather, in this instance, to follow these Versions, than to copy after the errors of the Bishops-Bible. —Acts XII. 16.

"For all the Athenians and strangers *which* [who] were there, spent their time in nothing else, but either *to tell or hear* [in telling or hearing] some new thing." It is rather better rendered in Tomson's, and in the Geneva Bible: "For all the Athenians and strangers which dwelt there, gave themselves to nothing els, but either to tell, or to heare some newes." —XVII. 21.

"*And as Paul was to be led* [And while they were conducting Paul] into the castle, he said &c." It does not appear from these words in our Version, that Paul was *actually* conducted into the Castle. It is rendered by Coverdale: "And whan Paul *began* to be caryed;" and in Tomson's, and in the Geneva Bible: "As Paul *should have bin led*." These are strange interpretations; but hardly more exceptionable than that by Mr. Wynne: "But as Paul *was going* to be brought &c." —XXI. 37.

"But when I found that he had committed nothing worthy of death, and that he himself had appealed to Augustus, *I have determined* to send him." It should not be here in the Definite, but —XXV. 25.

in the Indefinite Paſt Time "I determined," juſt as it is in Coverdale. On the contrary, it is very well rendered by the Paſt Definite Time in the Geneva Bible, becauſe the Perfect Participle *had* is not uſed: "Yet have I founde nothing worthie of death that he hathe committed; nevertheles ſeing that he *hathe* appealed to Auguſtus, *I have determined* to ſend him."

II. *In reſpect to Adverbs.*

Biſhop Lowth remarks, that the Adverb, as its name imports, is generally placed cloſe or near to the word which it modifies or affects; and that its propriety and force depend on the poſition*. His Lordſhip has given no other example than that of the Adverb "*only:*" but the juſtneſs of the obſervation may certainly be applied to Adverbs in general. It will evidently appear, that *alſo* and *therefore* are frequently uſed by our Tranſlators with the greateſt impropriety. The Adverb *alſo*, in particular, is often miſplaced; often nugatory; and ſometimes it even deſtroys the ſenſe of the Original.

Matt. II. 8. "And he ſent them to Bethlehem, and ſaid, Go and ſearch diligently for the young child, and when ye have found him, bring me word *again, that I may come and worſhip him alſo.*" Biſhop Pearce ſaw, that the Adverb *alſo*, in this verſe, ought to refer to Herod; for the words of the Original are, ὁπως καγω ελθων &c. but our Tranſlators, by miſplacing it, have connected it with "the child Jeſus." Herod ſays to the wiſe men, "When ye have found him, bring me word, that I *alſo* (i. e. as well as you) may go and worſhip him." But our preſent Verſion conveys a very different

---

* Introduction to Engliſh grammar, p. 139.

different sense, and makes the Pronoun "him" emphatical, instead of "I," as if he had said "that I may go and worship Jesus, as well as worship others." The Vulgate, the Zurich Version, and Beza, have "ut *et ego* veniam et adorem eum." Castalio: "ut *ego queque* ad eum adorandum proficiscar." And Diodati: "acciochè *ancora io* venga, e l'adori." In short, all the translations, that have fallen within my notice, are free from this error, except the Bishops-Bible, and our present Version. In the Geneva Bible it is rendered thus: "that I may come *also*, and worship him;" and much after the same manner L'Enfant and Beausobre: "afin que j'aille *aussi* l'adorer." Though this perhaps is not intirely right; yet it does not make the child Jesus emphatical. Of all our old translators, Wicklif has rendered it with the greatest precision: "that *I also* come and worschipe him." The Spanish Version has "paraque yo venga y lo adore." The force of the particle καὶ in καγω is not here expressed, as it undoubtedly ought to have been; but it was better to omit it, than to insert it in an improper place.

"But I say unto you, that Elias is come already; and they Mat. XVII. *knew him not* [did not acknowledge him,] but did unto him what- 12. soever *they listed* [they pleased.] *Likewise shall also the Son of man suffer of them* [Thus shall the Son of man *also* suffer from them."] "Ουτως και ὁ υιος &c." I have here produced one out of many instances, where the Adverbs *likewise* and *also* are improperly linked together in the same member of a sentence.

"And when ye stand praying, forgive, if ye have aught against Mark XI. any: *that your Father also which is in heaven may forgive you your* 25. *trespasses.*" The former part of this verse will be considered, when we come to inquire into the necessity of literal translations: the latter

latter part of it is very ill rendered; for as the Adverb *alſo* is ſo placed, that it cannot poſſibly be connected with the Verb *forgive*, it introduces a new and ſtrange meaning. The ſenſe requires that it ſhould be thus altered: "that your Father who is in heaven may *alſo* forgive you your treſpaſſes."

Luke VI. 13. "And when it was day, he called unto him his diſciples, *and of them he choſe twelve, whom alſo he named Apoſtles.*" The ſenſe of this verſe in our tranſlation ſeems to imply, that Jeſus had named other Apoſtles, beſide thoſe twelve whom he had then choſen; whereas had it been rendered " and *out* of them he choſe twelve, whom he named Apoſtles *alſo*," the true meaning would have been obvious.

—— X. 39. "And ſhe had a ſiſter called Mary, *which alſo ſat* at Jeſus's feet, and heard his word." It ſhould be " who *even* ſat;" for " *alſo*" ſeems to ſuggeſt, that others, as well as Mary, ſat at his feet.

—— XVIII. 15. "And they brought unto him *alſo infants* [infants alſo,] that he *would* [might] touch them." I have already conſidered this verſe upon another occaſion. It is obvious, that the Adverb *alſo* is miſplaced here; it ſhould follow the word " infants," and not precede it; for ſince it uſually throws the emphaſis upon the word immediately going before, it intirely alters the meaning of the paſſage. Here it would imply, that infants were brought to others as well as Jeſus, which doubtleſs is not the true ſenſe of it. We find the ſame in Cranmer's, and in the Biſhops-Bible, as in our preſent Verſion; but it is rendered properly by Coverdale: " They broughte *yonge children alſo* unto him, that he ſhoulde touche them."

—— XXIII. 32. "And there were *alſo* two *other* malefactors led with him to be put to death." This probably is the moſt exceptionable render-

ing

ing in the four Gospels. Every one just initiated in the principles of the English grammar must perceive, that the two words *also* and *other*, as they stand in our present Version, necessarily indicate, that our Blessed Lord was a malefactor, as well as the thieves who were crucified with him. But if we substitute *others* for *other*, and place *also* close to the Verb, there will be no obscurity or ambiguity: " And two *others*, who were malefactors, were *also* led with him to be put to death. The Geneva Bible, and the Bishops-Bible (the first of which is cited upon this occasion by Bishop Pearce) are not liable to the least exception in this respect; for we find in the former " and there were two *others*, which were evil doers, led with him to be slayne," and in the latter " and there were two evyll doers, led with him to be slayne." Tyndal, and Coverdale, and Cranmer have rendered it after the same manner. King James's translators were probably led into this gross error by the Vulgate: " Ducebantur autem et alii duo nequam cum eo, ut interficerentur," and this interpretation has been implicitly followed in the Syriac, Arabic, and Æthiopic Versions, as we learn from the Latin translations of them in the Polyglot; but the Persic Version gives us the true meaning of this verse: " et duos latrones facinorosos adducebant, ut illos etiam cum eo in crucem agerent." Wicklif has adhered to the Vulgate: " Also othere tweie wickid men weren led with him to be slayn," and we find the same kind of rendering in the Rhemish N. T. and even in the recent translation by Mr. Purver. This verse in the Original stands thus: " Ηγοντο δε και ετεροι δυο κακεργοι συν αυτω αναιρεθηναι." Henry Stephens first proposed to put κακεργοι between commas, that it might not be understood *joint malefactors with him*. Mr. Bowyer in his edition hath inserted it between commas; and

and Dr. Priestley hath with great propriety and judgement adopted the same method in his English Version*: " And there were also two *others*, malefactors, led with him to be put to death." Indeed I have often wondered, that any translators could possibly be induced to imagine, that the Evangelist meant to call Jesus κακεργος: for he has taken pains, as it were, in the very next verse to discriminate the sufferers, by pointedly saying, αυτον, και της κακεργες. I have been the more particular in examining this text, because it carries in it such an air of impiety that every well-meaning Christian must acknowledge, that it calls loudly for amendment.

Acts XI. 18. " When they heard these things, they *held their peace* [made no reply] and glorified God, saying, Then hath God *also* to the Gentiles granted repentance unto life." Every one must see that the words in this verse should have been placed thus: " Then hath God granted to the *Gentiles also* repentance unto life." How different is the sense, when, by the misplacing of *also*, the emphasis is laid upon the word *God?* It is very exactly rendered in the Rhemish N. T. " God then to the *Gentiles also* hath granted repentance unto life." So in the Zurich Version: " Nempe etiam gentibus Deus resipiscentiam dedit ad vitam." Thus likewise in the Italian Version: " Iddio ha dunque ha data la penitenza etiandio a' Gentili, per ottener vita." And in the same manner in the Spanish: " Demanera que tambien à las Gentes hà dado Dios penitencia para vida."

— XIII. 9. " Then Saul (*who also* is called Paul,) filled with the Holy Ghost, set his eyes on him." Were there any persons alluded to by St. Luke, beside Saul, who were called Paul? Our present Version

---

* English Harmony, p. 240.

fion fuggefts that there were, by mifplacing *alfo*. It ought to be "who is called *Paul alfo*."

"And when there was an affault made both *of* [by] the Gentiles, and *alfo of* [by] the Jews &c." I have blotted out "*alfo*," which is quite unneceffary after "*both*." Acts XIV. 5.

"For the king *knoweth of* [knoweth] thefe things, *before whom alfo I fpeak freely; for I am perfuaded* [being perfuaded] that none of thefe things are hidden from him, for *this thing* [this] was not done in a corner." St. Paul was very ready to appeal for the truth of his proofs to Agrippa, becaufe he knew him to be verfed in all queftions that refpected the Jews; for which reafon St. Paul fays " προς ὸν και παρρησιαζομενος λαλω," whence it is evident, that the Particle και has an illative fenfe, (of which there are many inftances in the N. T.) and that it ought to be rendered *therefore:* " before whom *therefore* I fpeak freely." Our Tranflators have utterly mifreprefented St. Paul's meaning; for the Adverb *alfo* implies, that he afferted, he fpake with freedom before Agrippa, as well as before others. It is obfervable, that no tranflations, which I have confulted, have given us the juft meaning of this Particle, except thofe by Caftalio and Tremellius. We read in the former: " Scit hæc rex, ad quem *eò* confidentius loquor, quod cum nihil horum latere perfuafum habeo." In the latter: " Et etiam rex Agrippa valdè novit de his ipfis quod ita fe habeant; et *idcirco* liberè loquor coram eo." —XXVI. 26.

As in the preceding inftance our Tranflators neglected to ufe an illative Particle, when it was requifite, fo on many occafions they have ufed one with impropriety. This appears particularly in Ουν, which fometimes is an expletive: fometimes a fimple conjunction; and fometimes an adverfative, as well as an illative

Particle. I shall give two or three examples of bad rendering in the latter sense.

<small>Matth. X. 25.</small> "It is enough for the disciple, that he be as his master; and the servant as his lord: if they have called the master of the house Beelzebub, how much more shall they call *them* [those so who are] of his houshold? (26) Fear them not *therefore* &c." Could our Saviour mean, that the reason why his Apostles had no just grounds of fear, was because they were sure to meet with barbarous treatment? Impossible: yet the Adverb "therefore" imports it. What our Saviour designed to inculcate, was evidently this; that they ought not to be alarmed by any apprehensions, because they would triumph hereafter in the justice of their cause. Ουν is plainly an adversative Particle, and should be rendered thus: "*Nevertheless* fear them not; for there is nothing covered, that shall not be revealed; *and hid* [nor hidden] that shall not be known." Our Translators have properly rendered μη ουν φοβηθητε in the 31st verse "fear ye not *therefore*," because Jesus had just informed his Apostles, that they were constantly under the immediate providence of God.

<small>Mark XII. 6.</small> "Having yet *therefore* one son, his well-beloved, he sent him also last unto them, saying, They will reverence my son." There ought not to be an illative Particle here: at least, not in that member of the sentence in which it is put; but probably ουν is an expletive; and it seems to be rightly omitted by Tyndal: "Yet had he one sonne, whom he loved tenderlye." "Ετι ουν ενα υιον εχων αγαπητον αυτε." And it is omitted likewise by Coverdale, Mathew, and Taverner.

<small>Luke XX. 29.</small> "There were *therefore* seven brethren, and the first took a wife, and died without children." It is said in the preceding verse, that

Moses

Moses ordered, that if a man died without children, his brother should marry his widow. Could this be a reason, why there should be *seven brethren?* Our present Version actually implies it, merely from an injudicious use of the illative Particle *therefore*. But ευ is here no more than a simple Conjunction, and should be rendered " now," just as in Tomson's, and in the Geneva Bible: " *Now* there were seven brethren."

" And Simon Peter stood and warmed himself: they said *therefore* unto him, Art not thou also one of his disciples?" The poor Particle *therefore* was never more miserably abused than in this verse. We should either substitute *then* for *therefore*, which has been done by Coverdale and Cranmer, and which is necessary in many other passages; or we should consider ευ as a Conjunction, after the manner of some of our old Versions: " And Simon Peter stood, and warmed himself; *and* they said unto him &c."

John XVIII. 25.

Sometimes Adverbs are used, when the nature of the English idiom requires the Personal Possessive; of which I shall content myself with mentioning one instance.

" And they *that* [who] had laid hold on Jesus, led him away to Caiaphas the high priest, *where* the scribes and the elders were assembled." It ought to be " in *whose* house," or, " in *whose* palace;" for, in this case, the Adverb ὁπου will not admit of being rendered literally by " *where*."

Matth. XXVI. 57.

I shall close my remarks upon the Adverbs by producing three instances of an improper use of the Adverb " *again*."

" And he sent them to Bethlehem, and said, Go, and search diligently for the young child, and when ye have found him, bring me word *again* &c." Does not this indicate, that they had brought him word *before?* Yet it is certain, that Herod employed

— II. 8.

the wife men but once upon this errand. The words of the Original are, απαγγειλατε μοι, "denunciate mihi," as in Beza; and "certiorem me facitote," as in Castalio; and indeed all the Versions are right in this particular, except a few of the old English ones; but Tyndal, Mathew, and Taverner render it "bring me word," and the Rhemish N. T. "make reporte to me."

Matt. XI. 4. "Jesus answered, and said unto them, Go, and *shew John again* those things which ye do hear and see." Did the Baptist send *two* messages to our Saviour? or did our Saviour charge the disciples of the Baptist with *two* answers to his questions? Undoubtedly not. We should therefore with Mr. Wakefield render πορευθεντες απαγγειλατε Ιωαννη "Go and *inform* John." Tyndal, Mathew, and Taverner, have judiciously omitted the Adverb "*again*" "Go and shewe John."

John IV. 54. "This is *again* the second miracle that Jesus did, *when he was* [after he had] come out of Judea into Galilee." That is, in plain English, the second miracle was wrought twice. Beza was aware of the consequence that would flow from this absurd interpretation of παλιν, and therefore qualified it in the following manner: "Hoc rursus, id est, secundum signum edidit Jesus &c." But it does not seem necessary either to have recourse to this method; or to look upon παλιν as an expletive, as some translators have done; or, with Bishop Pearce, to join παλιν to ελθων: we may render it by *porro*, *moreover*, in which sense it is sometimes used by the LXX, according to Mintert.

III. *In*

III. *In respect to Prepositions and Conjunctions.*

"Thy will be done *in* [on] earth, as it is in heaven." So Matth. IV. 6. επι των χειρων should be rendered "*on* their hands," not "*in* their hands;" and to the same purport in a variety of passages. — Matth. VI. 10.

"But when the people were put *forth* [put *out*, or, turned out] &c." So Acts V. 34. "and commanded to put the Apostles *forth a little space.*" It should be "and commanded the Apostles to be put *out for a little time.*" — IX. 25.

"And they were offended *in him.*" It ought to be "*at him*," as in Coverdale.——It will not be improper here to speak of the manner, though it hath often been remarked, in which king James's translators have rendered σκανδαλιζει in ch. V. 29, 30. and in other passages. "If thy right eye *offend* thee, pluck it out,—and if thy right hand *offend* thee, cut it off." These translators looked upon themselves as authorized to insert nonsense into the text, provided they foisted the true meaning into the margin; for we find in it this reading "cause thee to offend." But ought they not rather to have rendered it in the text "make thee to offend," or, "cause thee to offend," (as, in fact, it is in the Geneva Bible) than to affect the parade of a marginal note, which would be consulted by very few readers? So Matth. XVIII. 6. "*Whoso shall offend one of these little ones.*" If it had been translated thus: "*Whosoever* shall *cause* one of these little ones *to offend,*" it might be easily understood by the common people; whereas they must now take it in a sense directly opposite. Σκανδαλιζει has been properly rendered by Beza, and by the author of the Zurich Ver- — XIII. 57.

Verfion: "facit ut tu offendas." And by Schmidius: "te facit offendere." Not unlike this is the Verfion of Mons: "eft un fujet de fcandale et de chute." And the Italian Verfion: "ti fa intoppare." And alfo the Spanifh: te fuére ocafion de caer." The Vulgate has "fcandalizat;" but in what Claffical mint this expreffion was coined, I have not the good fortune to know.

Matt. XIX. 28.
"And Jefus faid unto them, Verily I fay unto you, that ye *which* [who] have followed me *in the regeneration, when the Son of man fhall fit in the throne of his glory, ye alfo fhall fit* [fhall, in the regeneration, when the Son of man fhall fit *upon* the throne of his glory, fit alfo *upon* twelve thrones &c."] King James's tranflators, in imitation of their predeceffors, have rendered here in the fame verfe "*in* the throne," and "*upon* the throne," as if they had a right to ufe Prepofitions at pleafure; but "*upon*" is undoubtedly moft proper. They probably thought themfelves authorized by the Vulgate, which has both "*in* fede" and "*fuper fedes.*" I have followed Bengelius, and others, in connecting καθισεσθε with εν τη παλινγενεσια, though one may juftly fufpect with Dr. Owen, that the three laft Greek words were thrown into the margin by fome perfon, who adopted the fanciful doctrine of a Millennium.

—XXIV. 48.
"*But and if that evil fervant* [But if that fervant who is wicked] fhall fay in his heart, *my lord* [my mafter] delayeth his coming." There are other paffages which ought to be corrected, in which the words *but and if* are joined together after the fame manner. They occur in Tyndal, Coverdale, and in the Bifhops-Bible; but in Tomfon's, and in the Geneva Bible, the verfe is thus rendered: "*But if* that evil fervant fhall fay in his heart, my *mafter* doth defer his coming."

"And

"And he afked his father, How long is it ago fince this came unto him? And he faid, *Of a child* [from his childhood."] Mark IX. 21.

"For all they did caft in *of their* [out of their] abundance; but fhe *of her want* [out of what fhe wanted for herfelf] did caft in all that fhe had, even all her *living* [fubftance."] — XII. 44.

"And they faid among themfelves, who fhall roll *us away the ftone* [away the ftone *for* us] from the door of the fepulchre?" — XVI. 3.

"When once the mafter of the houfe is rifen up, and hath *fhut to the door* [fhut the door &c."] Coverdale renders it " and hath fhut the dore," as it is likewife in the Rhemifh N. T. It is thus in Wicklif: " For whanne the houfbonde man is entrid, and the dore is clofed." Luke XIII. 25.

"For if they do thefe things *in* a green tree, what fhall be done *in* the dry?" To do a thing *in* a tree, feems to be rather a novelty; yet we find it in the Bifhops-Bible, and in Mr. Purver's Verfion. Our early tranflators more judicioufly ufed the Prepofition *to*, not *in*. — XXIII. 31.

"Now when he was in Jerufalem, at the paffover, *in* the feaftday &c." It fhould be either " *upon* the feaft-day," or " during the whole time of the feaft," which Dr. Clarke recommends. John II. 23.

"*The neighbours therefore* [Now the neighbours] and they *which* [who] before had feen him, *that* he was blind, faid, Is not this he *that* [who] fat and begged?" The Adverb *when* feems much more proper here than the Conjunction *that*; and it is rendered in moft of our antient Bibles " *when* he was blind." Beza makes the following obfervation upon this verfe: " Si pro ὅτι legas ὅτε, id eft, quum, planior etiam erit fententia; fed ex conjectura nihil placet mutare." Had Beza confulted the Septuagint Verfion, he would have found, than an alteration was unneceffary; for it appears from — IX. 8.

from Mintert, that ἐπι is sometimes used by the LXX to signify *quando, quum.*

Acts V. 40. " And *to him* [with him] they agreed &c."

—VI. 14. " For we have heard him say, that this Jesus of Nazareth shall destroy this place, and shall change the customs which Moses *delivered us.*" This is obviously very incorrect; for *delivered us,* without a Preposition, suggests a meaning widely different from what our Translators intended; it either should be " delivered *to* us," or, " gave us," as in many of our antient Bibles.

—VII. 39. " *To whom* [whom] our fathers would not obey &c." Why was not the Preposition omitted in this verse, as well as in V. 36. in which it is rendered " and all, as many as *obeyed him.*"

—XXVI. 31. " And when they were gone aside, they talked *between* [among] themselves &c." It appears, that Agrippa had a conference with all those who had sitten with him. Coverdale renders ελαλευ προς αλληλυς " talked together."

I have confined myself to a very few examples upon this head; and have avoided taking notice of the Conjunction Copulative *and*; for it would have been a tedious, if not an endless attempt; there being probably not fewer than two hundred passages in the four Gospels, where sentences are connected by this Conjunction, which ought to have been disjoined; and in which, of course, the sense is sometimes materially affected by it. A curious instance in this kind may be seen in the ninth chapter of St. Luke, consisting of sixty-two verses; forty-one of which begin with the Conjunction *and*. Whoever is desirous of understanding the nature and application of Prepositions and Conjunctions, would do well to read with attention a very ingenious dialogue written expressly upon this subject; the author of which appears to have a

com-

comprehensive knowledge of language in general, as well as of the force and propriety of the English tongue in particular *.

IV. *Where the Pronouns are either superfluous, or deficient, or ungrammatical.*

Bishop Lowth, after citing the following passage from Archbishop Tillotson, " *Who*, instead of going about doing good, *they* are perpetually intent upon doing mischief," observes, that the Nominative Case *they* in this sentence is superfluous, as it was expressed before in the Relative *who* †. Upon the strength of this remark I shall point out some similar passages in Scripture which require correction; and at the same time I shall take occasion to speak of other defects in regard to the Pronouns.

" But Jesus turned *him* about, and when he saw her &c." It should be " *himself*," the Reciprocal Pronoun. The same alteration should be made in other passages. There is no ambiguity in this verse, because Jesus spake to a woman; but it is otherwise in Luke VII. 9. " When Jesus heard these things, he marvelled at him, and turned *him* about, and said &c. One would imagine, that Jesus did not turn *himself* about, but the centurion, or one of the centurion's friends.   *Matth.* IX. 22.

" He *that* [who] loveth father or mother more than me is not worthy of me: and he *that* [who] loveth son or daughter more than me is not worthy of me." It would be better to supply here the Pronoun Possessive, viz. *his* father or mother, *his* son or daughter, as it has been done by Tyndal, Mathew, and Taverner.   —— X. 37.

" And brought the ass and the colt, and put on them their clothes,   ——XXI. 7.

L

---
* See Επεα Πτεροεντα, or the Diversions of Purley.
† Introduction to English grammar, p. 148.

clothes, and *they* set him thereon." The superfluous Pronoun *they* is not in the greater part of the old Bibles.

Matt. XXI. 17.
"And he left them, and went out of the city into Bethany, and *he* lodged there." Nor is this superfluous Pronoun in many of the antient Versions.

— XXIII. 34.
"Wherefore, behold! I send unto you *prophets* [teachers] and wise men, and scribes; and some of them ye *shall* [will] kill and crucify; and some of them *shall ye* [ye will] scourge in your synagogues, and persecute *them* from city to city." Here our Translators have inserted *them* in Italics, which was judiciously omitted by Tyndal, and by the authors of the Geneva Bible.

— XXV. 11.
"Afterward came also the other virgins, saying, Lord, Lord, *open to us*." Here the Pronoun is very improperly left out. We should render these words "open *it for* us," because it was said in the preceding verse, that the door was shut. — So Acts V. 23. "*The prison truly found we* [We indeed found the prison] shut with all safety; and the keepers standing without before the door; but when we had *opened*, we found no man within." It either should be "but when we had opened *it*," or "*which* after we had opened."

Mark V. 19.
"*Howbeit* [However] Jesus suffered him not, but *faith* [said] unto him, Go home to thy friends, and tell them, how great things the Lord hath done for thee, *and hath* had compassion on thee." In this verse more than the Pronoun *he* seems to be wanted. It should be "and *that he* hath &c." for the preceding Adverb *how* belongs solely to the Adjective. In one very antient MS. is ἐπι ηλεησε, which Beza has followed; and which seems to be the true reading.

— VII. 15.
"There is nothing from without a man that entering into him can

can defile him; but the things which come out of him, *those are they* that defile *the* [a] man." Surely this reduplication is unnecessary; and if it had been rendered "the things which come out of him defile him" the sense would have been preserved; but if we translate εκεινα εστι more literally, it should be either "are they," or, "are those," as in Tyndal, and in the Geneva Bible.

"And he took him aside from the multitude, and put his finger into his ears, *and he spit*, and touched his tongue." It ought to be "and spat," the Pronoun being needless, and not in the Bible above-mentioned. — Mark VII. 33.

"In the resurrection therefore, when they shall rise, whose wife shall she be *of them?*" The two last words are plainly redundant. — XII. 23.

"And Peter followed him afar off, even unto the palace of the high priest; and *he* sat &c." Here *he* is not only superfluous, but almost sufficient to create an ambiguity. It is neither in Tomson's, nor in the Geneva Bible. — XIV. 54.

"And he closed the book, and *he* gave it again to the minister, and sat down &c." *He* is superfluous here, as in the foregoing verse, and is not in the Bibles which I have just cited, nor in many other of the antient ones. — Luke IV. 20.

"And they were all amazed, and *they* glorified God." It is in the Geneva Bible: "And they were all amazed, and praised God." — V. 26.

"For whosoever shall be ashamed of me, and of my words, of him shall the Son of man be ashamed, when he shall come in his own glory, *and in his Father's*, and of the holy angels." Here the Pronominal Adjective had better be supplied: and in *that* of his Father, and of the holy angels." There is no incorrectness, however, in the Geneva Bible, in which the Substantive is repeated — IX. 26.

"and

"and in the glory of the Father &c." In the same manner the Substantive is repeated in almost all our old English Versions.

Luke XIII. 15.
"The Lord then answered him, and said, Thou hypocrite, doth not *each one* of you on the sabbath loose his ox or his ass from the stall &c." It should be either "each of you," or "every one of you." Coverdale has rendered it by the last Distributive Pronominal Adjective "doeth not *every one* of you loose his oxe or asse &c."

—-XX. 29.
"*There were therefore* [Now there were] seven brethren; and the first took a wife, and died without children. (30) And the second took her to wife, and *he* died childless." Can we imagine, that the Pronoun was necessary in the 30th, if it was not so in the 29th verse? And was there any reasonable ground for our Translators to render αυτος differently in these two verses? The Vulgate has "sine filiis" in both, as Beza has "sine liberis."

John I. 33.
"And I knew him not; but he *that* [who] sent me to baptize with water, the same said unto me, Upon *whom* thou shalt see the Spirit descending and remaining on *him*, the same is he *which* [who] baptizeth with the Holy Ghost." As the Pronoun "him" was expressed before in the Relative *whom*, it cannot but appear to be redundant.

—— —— 36.
"And looking upon Jesus as he walked, he saith, Behold the Lamb of God. (37) And the two disciples heard him speak, and *they* followed Jesus." In the Geneva Bible it is thus rendered: "And he behelde Jesus walking by, and said, Beholde the Lamb of God. And the two disciples heard him speake, and followed Jesus." Here is no useless Pronoun; and it is manifest, that Jesus was walking; whereas it does not appear clearly from our present Version, whether it were Jesus, or John.

"Jesus

"Jesus answered them, I told you, and ye believed not: the works that I do in my Father's name, *they* bear witness of me." I have seen no antient English Version, except that by Wicklif, in which the Pronoun is omitted: "the workis that I do in the name of my fadir beren witnessing of me." And it is to be remarked, that Wicklif seems to be more accurate in general than king James's translators, in the use of Pronouns. — John X. 25.

"The God of Abraham, of Isaac, and of Jacob, the God of our fathers hath glorified his Son Jesus; *whom* ye delivered up, and denied *him* in the presence of Pilate, when he was determined to let him go." The Pronoun *him* is liable to the same objection as in John I. 33. — Acts III. 13.

"*Him* God raised up the third day, and shewed *him* openly." The Geneva Bible hath "Him God raised up the third day, and caused that he was shewed openly." This certainly is harsh, being a literal rendering of the Original και εδωκεν αυτον εμφανη γενεσθαι, but there is nothing ungrammatical in it, as in our present Version. — X. 40.

"And he began to speak boldly in the synagogue: *whom* when Aquila and Priscilla had heard, they took *him* unto them, and expounded unto him the way of God more perfectly." Here again there are two Objective Cases "whom" and "him," the last of which is superfluous. Bishop Sherlock supposed, that, in the foregoing verse, the word *ουκ* had been omitted; and that we ought to read, εδιδασκεν ΟΥΚ ακριβως, "he taught the doctrine of Christ NOT perfectly, knowing ONLY the baptism of John*." The conjecture is doubtless ingenious; but it may be much questioned, whether it be necessary; especially if we include the begin- — XVIII. 26.

---

* Bowyer's Critical Conjectures &c. p. 256.

beginning of the 26th verse in the 25th. "This man was instructed in the way of the Lord; and, being fervent in the spirit, spake and taught diligently the way of the Lord, though he knew only the baptism of John; and he began to speak boldly in the synagogue. (26) But after Aquila and Priscilla had heard him, they took him *to their house*, and expounded unto him the way of God more perfectly."

V. *Where the Definite Article* the *is improperly used.*

Matt. XI. 2. "Now when John had heard *in the prison* [in prison of the] works of Christ, he sent two of his disciples." It was not intended to mark any particular prison in which John was secured; therefore the Definite Article was inadmissible. Tyndal renders it "being in prison." And Coverdale is much more exact here than king James's translators: "Whan Ihon beinge *in pryson* herde *of* the workes of Chryste &c."

Mark II. 17. "When Jesus heard it, he *saith* [said] unto them, They *that are whole* [who are in good health] have no need of *the* physician, but they *that* [who] are sick &c." It should be "*a* physician;" for no particular one is pointed out in the Original, but only a physician indefinitely. Though our present Version is wrong in this instance, it is right in the parallel passage, Luke V. 31. whereas, on the contrary, the Rhemish N. T. is right in the first instance, and wrong in the last; and this is the case with most of our early translators, as to the use of the Articles; which evidently shews, that they were not directed by any uniform rule.

—-VII. 15. "There is nothing from without *a* man that entering into him can defile him; but the things which come out of him, *those are they*

they [are thofe] that defile *the* man." I produced this paffage juft above, in fpeaking of Pronouns; and now mention it with a view of fhewing the great inaccuracy in regard to the Articles; for both the Indefinite and Definite Articles are applied to *man* in the fame verfe, when the former only was admiffible. The parallel paffage in Matth. XV. 11. is free from this glaring inconfiftency; which is an additional proof, that king James's tranflators, like their predeceffors, ufed the Articles at random.

"*And when he was entered into the houfe from the people* [And when he had entered into *a* houfe, after he had left the people] his difciples afked him concerning the parable." The words εις οικον muft mean fome houfe indefinitely; for not any mention is made of a houfe before in this chapter; nor indeed in the preceding. On the contrary, εις οικιαν in the 29th verfe is very properly rendered by the Indefinite Article. Mark VII. 17.

"*And again he fent* [And he fent] another fervant; and they beat him alfo, and *entreated* [treated] him fhamefully, and fent him away empty. *And again* [And] he fent *the third*." It fhould be " *a* third ;" for no particular fervant is fpoken of definitely. Luke XX. 11.

"And when he had given him *licence* [leave] Paul ftood on the ftairs, and beckened *with the hand* unto the people." It fhould be " with *his* hand ;" for the nature of our language requires the Pronoun Poffeffive, inftead of the Definite Article. The fame correction fhould be made in Acts XXVI. 1. But we find τη χειρι in Acts XIII. 16. and την χειρα in Matth. XII. 49. properly rendered " *his* hand," not " the hand ;" all which evidently fhews, that king James's tranflators ufed Articles in an arbitrary manner. Acts XXI. 40.

I have not here taken notice of one circumftance which often occurs; that is, the prefixing of the Definite Article to the Relative,

tive, as "*the which.*" This is certainly both harsh and incorrect. We meet with the same fault, though less frequently, in the earlier Versions.

VI. *Where the Verb precedes in the Singular Number, when it ought to be in the Plural.*

Luke V. 9. " For he was astonished, and all *that* [who] were with him, at the draught of the fishes which they had taken: (10) And so *was also* [were also] James and John the sons of Zebedee, *which* [who] were partners with Simon &c." It is exceedingly strange, that our Translators did not see the necessity of rendering it " were also," as the two Nouns *sons* and *partners,* and the Verb *were* followed in the Plural Number; but the same gross inaccuracy is in all the old Versions, which I have examined, except in that by Coverdale: " And so *were* James and Jhon also the sonnes of Zebede."

—IX. 17. " And they did eat, and were all filled; and there *was* [were] taken up of fragments that remained to them, twelve baskets." Here again king James's translators chose rather to adopt the blunder of their predecessors, than to follow Coverdale, who had justly rendered it " and there *were* taken up." Bishop Pearce observed the incorrectness in Luke V. 9. but took no notice of that in IX. 17. which is equally, if not more flagrant.

I shall conclude my observations upon *ungrammatical passages,* with mentioning an instance of a Pronoun being used in the Plural, when the Substantive, with which it agrees, is in the Singular Number.

John XV. 6. " If a man abide not in me, he is cast *forth* [out] as a branch, and

and is withered; and men gather *them*, and cast *them* into the fire, and *they* are burned." One would be tempted to think, that our Translators confidered the Subftantive *branch* as a Noun of Multitude, which might have a Pronoun agreeing with it in the Plural, as well as in the Singular Number. The commentators are greatly divided about the propriety of reading αυτα or αυτο, for both are found in MSS. but whether we approve of one or the other, it is certain that our prefent Verfion ought to be corrected, fince there is a very grofs Solecifm in it. If we prefer αυτα, we fhould render κλημα as if it were in the Plural Number "branches," and retain the Pronouns *them* and *they*; but if we prefer αυτο, we fhould fubftitute the Neuter Pronoun *it* in the room of *them* and *they*. This feems to be the better reading; and has been adopted by Coverdale, Mathew, Taverner, and Tyndal; the laft of whom has rendered the verfe thus: " If a man bide not in me, he is caft forth as a braunche, and is wythered: and men gather it, and cafte it into the fire, and it burneth." We find the fame reading likewife in the Rhemifh Verfion of the N. T. " If any abide not in me, he *fhal* be caft forth as *the* branche, and *fhal* wither; and they fhall gather *him* up, and caft *him* into the fire, and *he* burneth." But it is evident, that the compilers of this Verfion have fallen here into two inaccuracies: firft, by rendering *branch* by the Definite Article; and, fecondly, by ufing the Perfonal Pronouns *he* and *him*, inftead of the Neuter Pronoun *it*. On the other hand, they have rendered εβληθη, and εξηρανθη, with more propriety, than any of our Englifh tranflators; for there is no doubt, that the Aorift is ufed here to exprefs the fenfe of Future Time, agreeably to the idiom of the Hebrew language. Thus the Vulgate: " mittetur foras, et arefcet." So Beza: " ftatim ut palmes arescet;" but he adds immediately " deinde *colliguntur isti palmites,*" a barbarism of which he would not have been guilty, if he had not been strangely prepossessed in favour of the reading αυτα. The Vulgate is followed by the Spanish Version: " *será echado fuera como mal pampano* &c." and likewise by the Version of Mons: " Celuy qui ne demeure pas en moy, *será* jetté dehors comme un sarment inutile; il *séchera,* & on le *ramassera* pour le jetter au feu, & le brûler."

CHAPTER VII.

Upon mean and vulgar Expressions.

AMONG several particulars recorded by Cicero of Antistius, who made a considerable figure in the Roman Forum, we meet with the following observation: " Verbis non ille quidem ornatis utebatur, sed tamen non abjectis [*]." I have often thought that this is extremely applicable to a translator of the Bible, who should endeavour to avoid a low phraseology, as well as a studied elegance of style. It is the privilege of the ancient languages to be secure from contracting any kind of meanness; whereas in those, which are now spoken, as soon as a word or phrase is familiarly used by the common people, it becomes unfashionable; and is often rigorously proscribed by the polite world: a circumstance,

[*] De claris oratoribus, § 63.

stance, which puts us upon the necessity of furnishing a constant supply, either by inventing new terms; or by transplanting such as are of a foreign growth into our own soil. Perhaps we are sometimes fastidiously nice in this respect; and are apt to hurt our language, whilst we pretend to refine it; but although an affectation of improvement is blameable, when it is carried too far, yet we ought not to be deterred from imparting to a Version of the Bible all the *real* advantages, which our language has received. I am far from insinuating, that there are many indelicate expressions in our present Version of the New Testament; or that our Translators are justly liable to censure for using them; for it is probable, that they adopted the same words and idioms, which were employed by the best writers of the age; but still it must be acknowledged, that those few blemishes should be removed; for since we find from experience, that, in common subjects, the force of a sentiment is often lessened, and even utterly destroyed, when a writer deviates into a meanness of language, we should be scrupulously careful to guard against it in a subject of the highest importance to mankind, a Version of the Holy Scriptures.

Purver has not only reprobated the phraseology of our present Version in general, but has published a formal catalogue of the words which he judged unworthy of a place in it. These are ranged under several classes, as " clownish, barbarous, base, hard, technical, and obsolete." It might well be expected, that so desperate a critic should be perfectly skilled in his native tongue; but the following specimens of his taste will shew, that he boldly usurped a province, for which he was totally unqualified. Matth. V. 22. " *Blockhead.*" Mark VIII. 11. " began *to query* with him."

him." XII. 4. "And him they stoned, *nay, broke his head.*" XIV. 65. "Nay, the officers *laid him on* with stripes." Luke XVI. 14. "They *sneered* at him." XXIII. 21. "They *bawled out* thus." XXIII. 23. "Yet they *lay on* with loud voices."

Such are the flowers with which Purver has so liberally adorned his boasted translation. From a vicious affectation of what is natural and easy, he sometimes falls into very gross indecencies; and even where he does not notoriously offend against the rules of delicacy, his style is more exceptionable than any of those parts of our present Version, which I am now going to examine.

Matth. IX. 19.
" And Jesus arose, and followed him, and *so did* his disciples." This trivial mode of expression " so did" is in Italics: how much better is the rendering in Tyndal, and in most of the old Bibles? " And Jesus arose, and followed him with his disciples." Should it not be thought to appear clearly enough to whom the Pronoun *his* refers, we might transpose the words thus: " And Jesus arose, and with his disciples followed him."

—XVII. 6.
" And when the disciples heard it, they fell on their faces, and were *sore* [exceedingly] afraid." The Adverb " sore" ought to be universally expunged.

—.XXIV. 25.
" Behold! I have *told you before* [foretold you these things."]

— — 46.
" Blessed [Happy] is that servant, whom his *Lord when he cometh* [master at his coming] shall find *so doing* [thus employed."]

—.XXVII. 14.
" And he answered *to never a word* [not even a single word."] It is in Tyndal, and Coverdale: " he answered nothing."

— — 39.
" And they *that* [who] passed by, reviled him, *wagging* [shaking] their heads."

— — 44.
" The thieves also *which* [who] were crucified with him, *cast the same in his teeth* [reproached him in the same manner."] The
Rhemish

Rhemish Version hath "and the self same thing, the thieves also who were crucified with him, *reproached* him withal."

"And for fear of him *the keepers did shake* [those who watched trembled] and became as dead men." This passage has been placed in a new light by Mr. Markland, who observes, that σεισμος εγενετο μεγας, ver. 2. does not mean that there had been an earthquake, but that there had been a great fear or trembling among the soldiers; and that St. Matthew, as if he had been aware of the possibility of mistaking the word σεισμος, put the meaning of it out of all doubt by adding, εσεισθησαν οι τηρουντες *.   Matth. XXVIII. 4.

"*And if this come to the governour's ears, we will persuade him, and secure you.*" Here seem to be three particulars objectionable within a very narrow compass. The first member of this compounded sentence is both vulgarly expressed, and ill-translated,—the second is ill-translated,—and the third is ambiguous.——Perhaps it would be better thus: "And if this come to a hearing before the governour, we will appease him, and bear you harmless." The literal rendering of the latter part of the sentence is "we will cause you to be without care or trouble," "ὑμας αμεριμνους ποιησομεν." It appears from Mintert, that πειθω is used by the LXX to signify "placo consilio, propitium facio," which seems to be the meaning in this verse. In the Geneva Bible it is thus rendered: "And if the governour heare of this, we will persuade him, and save you harmles." Tomson's Version is rather too paraphrastical, though more expressive of the true sense: "And if this matter come before the governour to be heard, we will persuade him, and so use the matter, that you shall not need to care."——It may be remarked here, that there are many passages in which the   —— 14.

Verb

---

* Bowyer's Critical Conjectures &c. p. 42.

Verb " to perfuade" ought to be altered. Acts XVIII. 4. " And he reafoned in the fynagogue every fabbath, and *perfuaded* the Jews and the Greeks." It fhould be " endeavoured to perfuade;" for we find, ver. 6. that St. Paul was oppofed with uncommon vehemence. So XIX. 8. " And he went into the fynagogue, and fpake boldly for the fpace of three months, difputing and *perfuading* the things concerning the kingdom of God." Here it fhould be " endeavouring to perfuade them of," becaufe it is faid in the following verfe " that divers were hardened and believed not." Thus again, XXVIII. 23. " to whom he expounded and teftified the kingdom of God, *perfuading them* [endeavouring to perfuade them] concerning Jefus &c." It appears from the next verfe, that, in this conference, fome of the Jews believed not, and were feverely reproached by St. Paul. The Verb " to perfuade " was ufed by our early writers in the fame fenfe, in which we at prefent ufe the Verb " to inculcate;" but I believe, that " perfuafion" now always implies " conviction" in the minds of thofe who are addreffed.

Mark I. 45.   " But he went out, and began to publifh it much, and to *blaze abroad* the matter." Διαφημίζειν had better been rendered " to report," or " to fpread abroad," as in Matth. IX. 31.

——III. 13.   " And he *goeth up into* [went up] a mountain, and *calleth unto him whom he would* [and called whom he approved of, or chofe."]

——V. 26.   " And had fuffered many things *of* [from] many phyficians, and had fpent all that fhe had, *and was nothing bettered*, [and had received no benefit] but rather grew worfe." We find not this coarfe phrafe " nothing bettered" in Tomfon's, and in the Geneva Bible, where it is rendered " and it availed her nothing, but

but she became muche worse." Purver has not in the least improved here upon our present Version: "Having also suffered many things by many physicians, and all which belonged to her being spent, yet she nothing profited, but *was got rather* to be worse."

"And he said unto her, Daughter, thy faith hath *made thee whole* [saved thee] go in peace, and *be whole of thy plague* [be healed of thy disease.]"   Mark V. 34.

"*Why make ye this ado* [Why are ye thus disturbed] and weep?"   —— 39.

"When Jesus saw that the people came running together, he rebuked the *foul* spirit." I should rather render it, as in the Geneva Bible, " the unclean spirit."   ——IX. 25.

"*And so it was* [And it happened] that while they were there, the days were accomplished that she should be delivered." Purver has injudiciously substituted " fully up" instead of " accomplished."   Luke II. 6.

"Whose fan is in his hand, and he will thoroughly *purge* [cleanse] his floor, and he will gather the wheat into his *garner* [granary.]" The Geneva Bible has " make clean his floor."   ——III. 17.

"*Let these sayings sink down into your ears*." [Mark these words diligently.] This is the rendering in Tomson's, and in the Geneva Bible, which has nothing mean in it, and yet is as forcible as that in our present Version.   ——IX. 44.

"Blessed is the womb that bare thee, and the *paps* [breasts] which thou hast sucked."   ——XI. 27.

"And when *the people were gathered thick together* [there was gathered together a great multitude of people.]"   —— 29.

"And when he had spent all, there arose *a mighty famine* in   ——XV. 14.

that land." Rather " a great famine," or, " a great dearth," as in most of our old Bibles.

Luke XVII. 31. " In that day, he *which* [who] shall be on the house-top, *and his stuff* [and his goods, or, having his goods] in his house, let him not come down to take *it* [them] away."

—XXI. 16. " And ye shall be betrayed both by parents, and brethren, and *kinsfolks* [relations."] Tyndal, and many other translators have " kinsmen," which is less vulgar than " kinsfolks."

——34. " And take heed to yourselves, lest at any time your hearts be overcharged with *surfeiting* [intemperance] and drunkenness, and cares of this life, *and so that day* come upon you unawares." It should be either " and that day," or, " and lest that day,"] as in the Geneva Bible.

John VII. 23. " Are ye angry *at* [with] me, because I have *made a man every whit whole* [perfectly healed a man on the Sabbath-day?" It is strangely rendered by Taverner: " because I have healed an hole man on the Sabbath daye."

——XI. 28. " *And when she had so said, she went her way* [And after she had spoken these words, she went away."]

——XXI. 11. " And *for all* [although] there were so many, yet was not the net broken." Thus the Rhemish Version: " And although they were so many, the nette was not broken."

Acts VII. 26. " And the next day he shewed himself unto them as they strove, and would have *set them at one again* [reconciled them."]

——VIII. 3. " As for Saul, he made havock of the church, entering into every house, *and haling men and women, committed them to prison* [and by force committed men and women to prison."] So Luke XII. 58. " lest he *hale thee* [carry thee by force] to the judge." In Tyndal's, and in Coverdale's Bibles, it is " drawe thee out,"

and

and in that of Geneva " bring thee," which terms, though not sufficiently expressive, are not so vulgar as the Verb " hale."

" *Giving out that himself was some great one* [pretending that he himself was some considerable person,"] or, as in Tyndal and Coverdale, " sayinge that he was a man that could do great thynges," or, as in the Geneva Bible, " saying that he himself was some great man." The reader will necessarily observe, that our present Version is inferior to those above-mentioned, in this instance. — Acts VIII. 9.

" *And was baptized, he and all his straightway* [And was immediately baptized with all his family."] Coverdale hath " And immediately was baptised, and al his housescholde." — XVI. 33.

" And the *more part* [greater part] knew not wherefore they were come together." So XXII. 2. " more silence" ought to be rendered by " greater silence." — XIX. 32.

" *And it came to pass, that after we had gotten from them* [After we had departed *from the elders of the church*."] Most of our antient Versions have the Participle " departed." —. XXI. 1.

" Who also hath *gone about* [endeavoured, or, attempted] to prophane the temple." So XXVI. 21. —. XXIV. 6.

CHAPTER VIII.

Upon obsolete and harsh Expressions.

AS a translator of the Bible should observe the just medium between a vulgar and humble style, so he should be particularly cautious, that it be not too much antiquated. It cannot be denied, that old words are calculated to add to the dignity of a subject, as they carry with them a certain kind of solemnity; but unless they be sparingly and judiciously used, the sense will be obscured by them, and become unintelligible to ordinary readers. If such expressions do not appear to be sufficiently clear of themselves, they should be excluded from Holy writ; and the advice given to orators by a great writer of antiquity should be steadily pursued: " Superest igitur consuetudo; nam fuerit pene ridiculum malle sermonem quo locuti sunt homines, quam quo loquuntur *."

On the other hand, it should be the business of a translator of the Bible to avoid a diction too much modernized; for though it may lie open to the level of all capacities, it may possibly have an air of littleness, incompatible with the grave simplicity of the Scriptures. Upon this principle we cannot but disapprove of the following mode of rendering by Purver: Matth. XIV. 14. " Upon which Jesus going out *saw much company.*" Again, John XVIII. 3. " Judas therefore having received *a regiment.*" XVIII. 12. " *So the regiment, the colonel* and officers took Jesus and bound him."

But

---

* Quinctil. lib. 1. § 6.

But we cannot be furprized to find a defect in Purver, which may be obferved in Dr. Waterland. This writer, (as quoted by Dr. Dodd from an interleaved Bible, wherein our Verfion is corrected throughout with his own hand, apparently with a view to a new tranflation) though learned and judicious in many of his remarks, hath in fome of his alterations imprudently adopted the ufe of modern expreffions. Acts XIX. 38. inftead of " the law is open, and there are deputies," he renders it " It is Term-time, and the judges are fitting." And in the fame chapter, ver. 40. " For we are in danger to be called in queftion for this day's uproar," he tranflates it " For we are in danger of being indicted for a riot on account of this day." The language of the law may indeed be called the language of the age; but to infert unneceffarily into a Verfion of the Scriptures, either legal terms, or any technical phrafes, is highly objectionable. I fhall produce another inftance only from Dr. Waterland, which is liable to a fimilar exception. He tranflates αἱμορροῦσα, Matth. IX. 20. " bloody flux," which, befide being a more indelicate expreffion than " iffue of blood" determines, perhaps, too decifively the nature of the woman's difeafe.

What has been faid in regard to the impropriety of obfolete expreffions, is equally applicable to the uncouth terms, with which almoft every page of our prefent Verfion abounds. This harfhnefs arifes partly from an injudicious choice of words and phrafes, and partly from a ftiff and awkard mode of arranging them. The maxim " Qui libenter audiunt, magis attendunt, et facilius credunt *" is as true in Divinity, as in Oratory. Had our Tranflators expreffed themfelves in an eafy and natural manner,

* Quinctil. lib. 8.

ner, they would have fixed more effectually the attention of their readers, and of course led them to a more frequent perusal of the Sacred Writings.

I cannot forbear making mention again of Purver, who, in his *Index Expurgatorius*, hath expunged a multitude of words derived from the Latin. Such are " *abstain, abstinence, access, addicted, adjure, affinity, amiable, apt, assented, asserted, assigned, austere, benevolence, clemency, compact, detain, dismiss, infamy, penury, propitiation, retain, subvert, tenor* &c." But not satisfied with declaring war against the Latin derivatives, he hath included in his tables of proscription the following words which are used by our best authors, as well as by king James's translators. These are " *accounted, allure, amends, beguile, dealt, dearth, dismayed, hallow, realm, relied, resort, tidings, upbraid, warfare, utmost and uttermost, wedlock* &c." As the reader is able to form a just idea of Purver's Version from the examples already adduced, it is unnecessary to enlarge upon this head; it will be sufficient to remark, that we find an unity of character preserved through the whole performance; and that every part of it, as well as the following instances, makes it difficult to determine, whether the style be more vulgar, than it is rude and barbarous. Matth. XX. 34. " So Jesus being moved with affection touched their eyes, *and those* followed him." XXI. 9. " Pray *save be* to the Son of David." Mark I. 35. " Afterwards *at the morning getting up long within night.*" XI. 33. " So they make answer to Jesus, We do not know. And Jesus *gives reply* to them." Luke X. 29. " And who is my neighbour? (30) Which Jesus *taking up* said." XXIII. 33. " At length when they were come away to a place called *the Scull one.*" John XII. 27. " O Father save me from this hour; but for the *foregoing* I am come to it."

I shall

I shall now proceed to point out a few instances of the obsolete and harsh expressions which are to be met with in our present Version; and, instead of considering them separately, I shall take them in the order in which they occur.

"*Was minded to put her away privily* [disposed, or determined to put her away privately.]" Matt. I. 19.

"But I say unto you, that whosoever shall put away his wife, *saving for the cause of fornication* [except in the case of fornication,]" or, except it be for fornication, as in most of our ancient Versions. — V. 32.

"If therefore thine eye be *single* [clear, or unhurt.] (23) But if thine eye be *evil* [hurt, or distempered.]" — VI. 22.

"And *when he sowed* [while he was sowing] some seeds fell by the *way's side* [side of the road,] and the *fowls* [birds] came, and *devoured them up* [devoured them.]" — XIII. 4.

"But he *that* [who] received the seed *into* [in] stoney places, the same is he *that* [who] heareth the word, *and anon with joy receiveth it* [and immediately receiveth it with joy.] (21) Yet hath he not root in himself; *but dureth for a while* [but lasteth only for a season,] or, endureth for a season," as in Coverdale — "for when tribulation or persecution ariseth because of the word, *by and by he is* [he is instantly] offended." — 20

"Then Jesus sent the multitude away, and went into *the* [a] house: and his disciples came unto him, saying, *Declare* [expound or, explain] unto us the parable of the tares of the field." — 36.

"Give ye them *to eat* [something to eat."] There are numberless passages in our present Version, where phrases in this kind require the words *some* or *something* to be supplied. The foregoing verse — XIV. 16.

verse is still rendered worse by Purver: "Do ye give them some to eat."

Mat. XXI. 24.
" I *in likewise* [in like manner, or, likewise] will tell you." The Geneva Bible hath " I likewise will tell you."

—— — 31.
" *Whether of them twain* [Which of the two] did the will of his father?" This mode of expression must be corrected in other places.

——XXII. 6.
" And the *remnant* [rest of them] took his servants, and *entreated them spitefully* [treated them reproachfully, or contemptuously] and slew them." Our Translators have not given the true meaning of ὕβρισαν, and the Verb " to entreat" is now obsolete in the sense in which they apply it.

—— — 20.
" Whose is this image and *superscription* [inscription."] We find " inscription" in the margin.

—— — 25.
" And the first, when he had married a wife, *deceased*." The Verb Neuter " to decease" is now obsolete. It is right in Coverdale: " The fyrst marryed a wyfe and dyed."

—. XXIV. 43.
" But *know this* [ye know this] that if the *good-man* [master] of the house had known *in what watch* [at what hour of the night] the thief would come, he would have watched, and would not have suffered his house to be *broken up* [broken into."] The Original has διορυγῆναι " to be digged through," after which manner it is rendered in some of our ancient Versions; but " broken into" seems more agreeable to our language. Luke XII. 39. διορυγῆναι is translated " to be broken through."

——XXV. 44.
" When saw we thee *an hungred, or a thirst* [hungry or thirsty."] It is in Coverdale: " When sawe we the hungree or thyrstie."

—. XXVI. 55.
" I sat daily with you teaching in the temple, and ye *laid no hold*

hold on me [did not lay hold on me, or, did not apprehend me."] The Geneva Bible hath " and ye toke me not."

" Surely thou alfo art one of them, for thy fpeech *bewrayeth* [betrayeth, or, difcovereth] thee." — Matth. XXVI. 73.

" And they had then a *notable* [notorious] prifoner, called Barabbas." — XXVII. 16.

" There cometh one mightier than I after me, the *latchet* [ftring] of whofe fhoes &c." — Mark I. 7.

" He faw a great multitude about them, and the Scribes *queftioning with them*." It would be better " difputing with them," as it is rendered by moft of our early tranflators. — IX. 14.

" And now the *even-tide* [evening] was come." In the Geneva Bible it is " And now it was evening." — XI. 11.

" And he faid unto them *in his doctrine* [in the courfe of his teaching,] Beware of the Scribes, *which* [who] love *to go in long clothing* [to walk in long garments."] — XII. 38.

" And they went and told it unto the *refidue, neither believed they them* [reft of the difciples, who yet did not believe them."] — XVI. 13.

" And the child grew, and *waxed ftrong* [was ftrengthened] in fpirit, and was in the deferts, *till the day of his fhewing unto Ifrael*." We cannot do better than to follow Tomfon's, and the Geneva Bible, in rendering the latter part of this verfe : " till the day came that he fhould fhew himfelf unto Ifrael." The whole verfe is well rendered in the Rhemifh Verfion : " And the child grew, and was ftrengthened in fpirit, and was in the deferts, until the day of his manifeftation to Ifrael."— So Luke XIII. 19. " and *waxed* a great tree ;" it would be better " and *became* a great tree." — Luke I. 8.

" And the people fought him, and came unto him, *and ftayed him*, — IV. 4.

him, that he should not depart [and pressed him to depart not] from them."

Luke VI. 4. " And when they had *this done* [done thus."]

— VII. 18. " And the disciples of John *shewed him of* [reported to him] all these things." The Verb " to shew" had better be altered in every verse, where it is used in the same sense, as " to tell," or, " to report."

— IX. 36. " And they kept it *close* [secret."]

— X. 40. " But Martha was *cumbred about much serving* [distracted or hurried with constant attendance."]

— XII. 19. " And I will say to my soul, Soul, thou hast *much* [many] goods laid up for many years."

— — 29. " *Neither be ye of doubtful mind.*" If this gave us the meaning of the words in the Original, μη μετεωριζετε, it must needs be esteemed harsh language; but it should be rendered " and be not in a state of anxious suspense," as Bishop Newcome hath observed in a note upon Hosea XI. 7.*

— — 58. " *Give diligence* [Be careful] that thou mayest be delivered from him."

— XIII. 18. " *And whereunto shall I resemble it?* [And to what shall I compare it?"] The Verb " to resemble" is seldom or never used now in an Active signification.

— XIV. 28. " For which of you intending to build a tower, sitteth not down first, and *counteth the cost* &c." Why should it not still more literally be translated? " calculateth the expense" ψηφιζει την δαπανην. This seems to be less harsh.

— XVII. 9. " Doth he thank that servant because he did the things commanded him? *I trow not* [I think, or, apprehend he will not."]

Dr.

* An attempt towards an improved Version &c. p. 73.

Dr. Owen very juftly remarks, that this anfwer appears both languid and needlefs after the interrogation; and he farther fays, that Ου δοκω is wanted in three MSS. and in the Coptic and Armenian Verfions.

"And he faid, All thefe *have I kept from my youth up* [I have kept, or, obferved from my youth."] The prepofterous Adverb "up" is neither in Tyndal, nor in Tomfon's, nor in the Geneva Bible. Luk. XVIII. 21.

"Who fhall not receive *manifold more*," Rather "much more," as in moft of our ancient Verfions. —— 30.

"And he called his ten fervants, and delivered *them* [to them] ten pounds, and faid unto them, *Occupy till I come.* [Trade, till I come."] Tyndal has rendered πραγματευσασθε much more properly "bye and fell." King James's tranflators have rendered rightly διεπραγματευσατο in the 15th verfe. —XIX. 13.

"And behold! there was a man named Jofeph, *a counfellor, and he was a good man and a juft*, [one of the council-chamber of the temple, a good and juft man."] So Mark VI. 20. "For Herod feared John, knowing he was a juft *man and an holy* [and holy man."] To put the Subftantive between the Adjectives, is very difagreeable to the ear. It is obfervable, that the Rhemifh Verfion, though for the moft part uncommonly harfh, is right in both thefe paffages. — XXIII. 50.

"Search the Scriptures, for in them ye think ye have eternal life, *and they are they which teftify of me* [and they bear teftimony of me, or, and they are the writings which bear teftimony of me."] John V. 39.

"The day following, when the people *which* [who] ftood on the other fide of the *fea* [lake] faw that there was *none other* [no other] —VI. 22.

	other] boat there, *save that one where into his disciples were entered* &c. [except that into which his disciples had entered &c."]
John VII. 4.	" For there is no man that doeth any thing in secret, and he himself seeketh to be known openly." It seems to be rendered better by Coverdale: " He that seketh to be openly knowen, doeth nothinge in secrete."
—XI. 56.	" Then sought they for Jesus, and *spake* [said] among themselves &c."
—XII. 6.	" This he said, not that he cared for the poor, but because he was a thief, and had the *bag* [purse], and *bare* [carried] what was put therein."
— — 9.	" *Much people of the Jews therefore* [Now many of the Jews] knew that he was there." The expression " much people" should be corrected throughout.
— — 24.	" Verily, verily, I say unto you, Except *a corn* [a grain] of wheat fall into the ground, and die, *it abideth alone* [it remaineth there a single grain."] This rendering by Dr. Heylin is much easier than " abideth alone."
—XVI. 25.	" These things have I spoken unto you in *proverbs*; the time cometh, when I shall no more speak unto you in *proverbs*, but I shall *shew you plainly of the Father* [clearly explain to you what relates to the Father."] Παροιμιαις ought to be rendered " parables," as in the Geneva Bible; but our Translators chose rather to thrust this interpretation into the margin, than to admit it into the text.
—. XXI. 7.	" *He girt his fisher's coat unto him.* [He girt on his fisher's coat."]
Act. III. 3.	" Who seeing Peter and John *about to go into the temple, asked an alms* [going towards the temple begged some alms."] " An alms" is now quite disused.

" And

" And they *took knowledge of them that they had been* [knew them   Acts IV. 13. to have been, or, knew that they had been] with Jesus."— So XVII. 13. " But when the Jews of Theffalonica *had knowledge* [knew] that the word of God was preached *of* [by] Paul &c." Tyndal, and Coverdale, and many others ufe the Verb " to know" inftead of the unharmonious phrafes " to take" and " to have knowledge."

" Neither was there *any among them that lacked* [a needy man   — — 34. among them."]

" Now when the high prieft, and the *captain of the temple*   — V. 24. [commander of the guard of the temple], and the chief priefts *heard* [heard of] thefe things, they doubted of *them whereunto this would grow* [the confequences of them."]

" And when he was full forty years old, it came into his *heart*   —VII. 23. [mind] to vifit his brethren the children of Ifrael." Coverdale renders it " came into his mind." The Vulgate hath " afcendit in *cor* ejus."

" And when Saul was come to Jerufalem, he *affayed* [endea-   —IX. 26. voured] to join himfelf to the difciples."

" And go with them *doubting nothing* [without any fcruple,"   —X. 20. or, " hefitation."]

" *Then prayed they him to tarry certain days* [Then they requefted   — — 48. him to continue with them fome time longer."]

" I was in the city of Joppa, praying, and in a trance *I faw*   —XI. 5. [faw] a vifion, a certain veffel *defcend as it had been* [defcending, as *if* it had been, or, in the form of] a great fheet, let down from heaven by four corners; and it came *even* [clofe] to me: (6) *Upon the which when I had faftened mine eyes, I confidered,* [And looking ftedfaftly upon it, I obferved] and faw &c." Our Tranflators have

have been guilty of the same inaccuracy, which has been above intimated; for X. 11. they rendered properly βευξει καταβαινον σκευος "saw a certain vessel *descending*," whereas XI. 5. they have used the Infinitive Mode instead of the Participle, ειδον καταβαινον σκευος "I saw a certain vessel *descend*." Coverdale uses the Participle "comminge down" in both verses; and the Geneva Bible is sufficiently exact in this particular; for it is rendered X. 11. "And he saw heaven opened, *and* a certain vessel *came down* unto him," and XI. 5. "I was in the city &c. and I saw a certain vessel *coming down* &c."

Acts XI. 13. "*And he shewed us how* [Who informed us that] he had seen an angel in his house, *which stood and said unto him* [who had said unto him]. send men to Joppa, and *call for* [inquire for] Simon, whose surname is Peter." So X. 5. we should substitute "inquire for" in the room of "call for."

—— XII. 9. "And he went out and followed him, and *wist not that it was true which was done by the angel* [knew not that what had been done by the angel was a real fact,] but thought he saw a vision." Ουκ ᾐδει is rendered both in Tomson's, and the Geneva Bible "knew not." So III. 17. "And now, brethren, *I wot* that through ignorance ye did it." It would be much better "I know," as in the two Bibles just mentioned.

—— —— 23. "*And he was eaten of worms, and gave up the ghost* [And being devoured by vermin, he expired."] It is rendered in the Geneva Bible "*so that* he was eaten of worms &c." which seems to describe the effect of the Angel's having smitten him. It is thus also in L'Enfant and Beausobre: "de *sorte* que mourut rongé des vers." See a judicious note upon this verse by Bishop Barrington in Bowyer's Critical Conjectures.

"Be-

"Behold! ye *despisers* [transgressors] and wonder, and *perish*, for I work a work in your days, *a work which you shall in no wise believe, though a man declare it unto you* [which ye will not believe, though it be evidently declared unto you."] Αφανισθητε is rendered in the Geneva Bible " vanish away." See Bishop Newcome's note upon Habakkuk I. 5. agreeably to which, I have rendered καταφρονηται " transgressors," and have not repeated the Substantive εργον, because there is very good authority for omitting it in the second instance; and, in fact, it is omitted by Tyndal, Coverdale, Mathew, and Taverner.

Acts XIII. 41.

" Then all the multitude kept silence, and *gave audience* [attended] to Barnabas and Paul, *declaring* [while they related] what miracles and wonders God had wrought among the Gentiles *by* [through] them."

—XV. 12.

" And after they had *tarried there a space, they were let go* [continued there some time, they were suffered to depart] in peace from the brethren unto the Apostles."

—— 33.

" And after he had seen the vision, *immediately we endeavoured* [we immediately endeavoured] to go into Macedonia, *assuredly gathering* [being assured, or, concluding] that the Lord had called us *for to preach* [to preach] the gospel unto them." The use of the Preposition *for* in this, and the like instances, before the Infinitive Mode, is quite obsolete. Tomson's and the Geneva Bible have " being assured" and " to preach" not " for to preach."

—XVI. 10.

" Wherefore I *take you to record*, [solemnly assure you] that I am pure from the blood of all men; (7) For *I have not shunned to declare unto you* [For I have kept nothing back, but have declared unto you] all the counsel of God." In many of our ancient Versions, Ου γαρ υπεστειλαμην is rendered " I have kept nothing back,"

—. XX. 26.

which

which is more literally, as well as more easily expressed than " I have not shunned."

Acts XX. 30.
" *Also of your own selves* [From among yourselves also] shall men arise &c." It is in Coverdale: " Yea, even from amonge youre own selfes shall men aryse."

—- XXI. 6.
" And when we had taken *our leave one with another* [leave of one another.*"*] In the Geneva Bible, " when we had embraced one another."

—— — 24.
" *Them take* [Take them] and purify thyself with them, *and be at charges* [at a joint expense] with them, that they may shave their heads." It is very well rendered in the Geneva Bible " contribute with them." On the contrary, " do coste on them," which is in the Bishops-Bible, is still more quaint than the rendering in our present Version.

—XXIII. 1.
" *Men and brethren* [Brethren] I have *lived in all good conscience* [always lived with a good conscience] before God, until this day."

—— — 12.
" And when it was day, *certain of the Jews banded together* &c. [some of the Jews conspired &c."] Purver has with reason rejected " banded together," but he has rendered ποιησαντες συςροφην " raising a mob," which is certainly more exceptionable.

—— — 15.
" Now therefore ye with the council signify to the *chief captain* [commander] that he bring him down unto you to morrow, as *though* [if] ye would inquire something more perfectly concerning him; and we, *or ever* [before] he come near, *are ready* [will be ready] to kill him." Or ever was frequently used by the writers of the last century in the same sense in which we use *before*, but it is now become obsolete.

—- XXIV. 28.
" But after two years Porcius Festus *came into Felix room* [succeeded Felix in his government,] and Felix willing *to shew the Jews*

Jews a pleasure, left Paul *bound* [in chains."] The words Χαριτας καταθεσθαι τοις Ιεδαιοις denote something more than to please the Jews; for it was done with a view of ingratiating himself with them; agreeably to which Beza renders it " volens gratiam inire a Judæis," and the authors of the Geneva Version " to get favour of the Jews." At any rate we should banish the uncouth phrase " to shew a pleasure."

" Now when Festus was come into the province, after three days, he *ascended* from Cæsarea to Jerusalem." It should be " went up," as in Coverdale, and in many other Versions. Acts XXV. 1.

" And when they had been there many days, Festus *declared Paul's cause* [explained Paul's case] unto the king, saying, There is a certain man left in *bonds* [chains] by Felix." —— 14.

" *At Festus commandment* [At, or, by the command of Festus] Paul was brought forth." —— 23.

" But he said, I am not mad, most noble Festus, but speak *forth* the words of truth and soberness." The Bishops-Bible hath " speake foorth," whence it probably came into our present Version; but the Adverb " forth," is omitted by Tyndal, and Coverdale, and many other translators. — XXVI. 25.

CHAPTER

CHAPTER IX.

Upon the Necessity of a literal Translation.

WE have now taken a general view of the qualifications necessary to a translator of the Bible. It has been my endeavour to shew, that he ought to convey the meaning of the Original with clearness and precision: that he should be competently versed in the principles of English Grammar: and that he should carefully avoid every word and idiom, which have a tendency to deform his language. We are in the last place to consider, whether he should translate literally or not. Much has been said on this subject by learned expositors of Scripture; but the examples of those, upon whose judgements we may safely rely, as well as many conclusions arising from the nature of the thing itself, lead me decisively to affirm, that a Version of the Bible should be as literal, as the difference of language will permit.

Though it should be allowed, merely for the sake of argument, that a loose translation may be of sufficient authority in determining matters of faith and practice, yet still it would be liable to an insuperable objection: I mean, the impossibility of furnishing the reader with a just idea of the Original. It is remarked by an ancient writer: "Ἑκάςε γαρ ὁν ιδιον τι, καλον εςιν. Ει δε τετο εναλλεξειας, ακαλλες το αυτο παρα την Χρησιν γιγνεται *." This observation is the result of good sense and experience. There is hardly
an

---

* Lucian. § 11. Πως δει την ιςοριαν συγγραφειν.

an author of real merit, who has not something which discriminates him from others: something in his manner of expressing himself, which he may claim to be his own; and if we endeavour to give a new air to any of his works, either by the length of periods, the copiousness of phrases, or the richness of imagery, we shall not only represent him intirely unlike himself, but shall probably injure the whole form and turn of his composition. Bishop Lowth has clearly proved this in respect to the poetical and prophetical parts of Scripture; and undoubtedly it is the case with the four Gospels. Where can we find a narrative so equal and uniform, and so peculiar in its kind? Here are no swelling or useless epithets: no laboured conceits or puerilities: no impertinent harangues or reflections: and not a single attempt to excite, much less to warm the passions. The story is related in so plain and artless a manner; so different from the admired productions of Greece and Rome; and yet so wonderfully affecting and persuasive, that the beautiful simplicity of it must necessarily be destroyed by adventitious embellishments.

As an attempt has been made in our language towards *a liberal translation*, which more properly should be called *a loose translation of the New Testament*, it will be of use to examine some passages, as evidences of what has been advanced. The author professes to have two points in view: "to discover the true sense of the Original; and to clothe his ideas in the vest of modern elegance." And he farther informs us, "that he imitated Castalio, who deserved well of mankind for translating the Scriptures in a pure, elegant, and *diffusive* style*." One could scarcely imagine, that Castalio was the pattern by which he had formed himself; for

* See Dr. Harwood's preface to his liberal translation.

Castalio's Version of the New Testament is remarkably concise, as the following contrast will evidently shew.

Present Version. *Liberal Translation*

Matth. III. 3.

The voice of one crying in the wilderness, Prepare ye the way of the Lord, make his paths strait. — It is the same in Mark I. 3. So Castalio: "Vox clamantis in solitudine, Parate viam Domini, rectas facite semitas ejus." — Mark I. 3. "dirigite semitas ejus" without any other difference.

Matth. III. 3.

Hark! the voice of a *public cryer* in the wilderness, Prepare a way for the Messiah, make an easy path for his sacred steps. — Mark I. 3. Hark! how the wilderness resounds with the loud proclamation! O prepare for the speedy advent of the Messiah. *Strew the path with flowers*, in which his sacred feet shall tread.

Though the Prophet introduces a harbinger giving orders to remove all obstacles in the wilderness, yet the expression "*public cryer*" seems to border upon the mean and vulgar; and "*to strew the path with flowers*" is a poetical image very ill adapted to the solemnity of the occasion.

Matth. IV. 16.

The people which sat in darkness saw great light; and to them *which* [who] sat in the region and shadow of death light is sprung up.

Matth. IV. 16.

Thine inhabitants who had long been involved in darkness, saw at once the *chearing beams of divine light burst upon them, which dispelled from thy regions the shades of that dense and uncomfortable obscurity* which once covered them.

What an affected Pleonasm is this! Castalio was content with rendering it as plainly, and almost as literally as king James's translators: "Populus in tenebris degens vidit lucem magnam, et manentibus in terræ noctis regione lux orta est."

Matth. VII. 16.

Do men gather grapes *of* [from] thorns, or figs *of* [from] thistles?

Matth. VII. 16.

Thorns produce not the *generous* grape — the thistle bears not the *luscious* fig.

To raise any sentence by epithets beyond what it is in the Original, especially if it be a kind of proverbial expression, is highly injudicious. Not so Castalio: Scilicet colligitur ex spinis uva, aut ex tribulis ficus?"

Matth.

Present Version. | *Liberal Translation.*

Matth. VIII. 3.
I will, be thou clean.

Matth. VIII. 3.
I will restore thee to health.

I need not point out the sublimity of Θελω, καθαρισθητι, which has been justly compared with the celebrated passage in the first chapter of Genesis, cited and commended by Longinus himself: the sublimity is preserved in our present Version, and in Castalio: "*Volo, mundus esto,*" but is intirely lost in the Liberal Translation.

Matth. XI. 28.
Come unto me all ye *that* [who] labour, and are *heavy* [heavily] laden, and I will give you rest.

Take my yoke upon you, and learn of me, for I am meek and lowly in heart: and ye shall find rest unto your souls.

For my yoke is easy, and my burthen is light.

Castalio.
Venite ad me omnes laborantes et onusti, et ego recreabo vos.

Subite jugum meum, et a me discite, qui mitis sum, et animo summissus, et invenietis animis vestris requiem.

Meum enim et jugum commodum, et onus leve est.

Matth. XI. 28.
Come unto me all ye who groan under the unsupportable burthen of the ceremonial law — and I will *vindicate you into perfect liberty and freedom.*

Obey my doctrines and precepts which I have *illustrated and enforced* by my own conduct; and learn from my examples of *inoffensive meekness and unaffected humility* — and you will secure true and lasting peace and happiness.

For my doctrine is calculated for the felicity of mankind — its injunctions are not rigorous and oppressive to human nature — but the paths into which it introduces men are *unspeakably pleasant and delectable.*

Had Dr. Harwood adhered as closely to the Original, as Castalio and king James's translators, he would not have weakened the force and effect of our Saviour's pathetic exhortation.

Matth. XX. 1.
For the kingdom of heaven is like unto *a man that is an housholder which* [a housholder who] went out early in the morning to hire labourers into his vineyard.

Castalio.
Perinde enim accidit in coelesti regno, ac in homine patrefamilias, qui exiit primo mane ad conducendum operarios in vineam suam.

Matth. XX. 1.
For the reception Christianity shall meet with at its first promulgation may be fitly represented by the following parable: — *Soon as the morning dawned,* a gentleman rose to hire day-labourers to work in his vineyard.

The phrase "*soon as the morning dawned*" seems much more fit for poetry, than for a plain narrative; and why ανθδωπος should be rendered "a gentleman" it is hard to conceive; for there is nothing in the Greek word which marks his rank in life. Besides, the term "gentleman" appears to be of too modern a cast to be admitted into Holy writ; and is therefore liable to the same exceptions, as several words and idioms already observed; to which we may add the following instances from Dr. Harwood. Luke XII. 16. "It happened that the immense estates of *an opulent gentleman* one year proved uncommonly fertile."—XIII. 6. "*A gentleman* had planted a fig-tree."—XV. 11. "*A gentleman of a splendid fortune and opulent* had two sons."—Thus likewise Joseph of Arimathea and Nicodemus are styled "*gentlemen.*" Instead of saying "The same came to Jesus by night" Dr. Harwood has thus rendered John III. 2. "*This gentleman privately stole to Jesus in the silence of the night.*"—Matth. XXVI. 47. "He had not spoken these words before Judas approached him, attended with *a vast mob* armed, some of them with swords, others with clubs, whom *the prelates and magistrates* had hired for this purpose." Mark V. 39. "*The young lady is not dead, but is only sunk into a profound sleep.*"—XII. 32. "*The clergyman* said to him, *You have given, Sir,* the only true and proper answer to the question." In other passages the Scribes are called "*the Jewish clergy*" and what is still more surprizing "*the inferior clergy.*"—Luke VIII. 1. "After this Jesus attended with his twelve disciples, *took a tour* through the towns and villages in those parts."—These, and numberless other expressions which equally partake of the familiarity of common discourse, are inconsistent with the uniform simplicity of the

Gospels;

Gospels; and when we admire with reason this quality in the Original, we cannot forbear condemning the neglect of it in a Translation.

Present Version.	*Liberal Translation.*
Matth. XXIII. 37.	Matth. XXIII. 37.
O Jerusalem, Jerusalem, thou that killest the prophets, and stonest them *which* [who] are sent unto thee, how often would I have gathered thy children together, even as a hen gathereth her chickens under her wings, and ye would not!	O Jerusalem, Jerusalem, who hast murdered so many prophets, and has stoned to death so many good men who were sent to reform thee,—for how many ages have I strove to save thee from ruin with all the anxious care and solicitude of the most affectionate parent!—but you have obstinately refused.

A man must be destitute of every tender feeling, who hesitates one moment to which of these Versions he should give the preference. Castalio's is strictly literal: " Hierosolyma, Hierosolyma, quæ vates occidis, et ad te missos lapidas, quoties volui congregare tuos natos, quomodo gallina suos pullos sub alas congregat, et noluistis!"

Matth. XXVI. 39.	Matth. XXVI. 39.
And he went a little further, and fell on his face, and prayed, saying, O my Father, if it be possible, let this cup pass from me: nevertheless not as I will, but as thou wilt. Castalio. Deinde paululum progressus, pronus procidit, et hunc in modum supplicavit: Mi pater, si fieri potest, fac ut effugiam hoc poculum: quanquam non ut ego volo, sed ut tu.	Having said this, he advanced a few steps from them,—prostrated himself on the ground, and uttered this prayer,—O merciful God! suffer not the impending stroke to break over my head;—*but I check myself.*—Not my will, but thine be done.

In the preceding quotation it is observable, that, in our Saviour's pathetic address to Jerusalem, Dr. Harwood omitted to render that most apposite and affecting comparison " ὃν τρόπον ἐπισυνάγει ὄρνις &c." whereas in the present instance he hath added this languid expression: " *But I check myself.*" To add unnecessarily

rily a single word to the discourses of our Blessed Lord, is as improper, as to omit any part of them.

Present Version.

Matth. XXVII. 61.
And there was Mary Magdalene, and the other Mary sitting over against the sepulchre.
Castalio.
Quum quidem illic esset Maria Magdalena, et altera Maria, e regione sepulchri sedentes.

Mark X. 24.
But Jesus answereth again, and saith unto them, Children, how hard is it for them *that* [who] trust in riches to enter into the kingdom of God!—Castalio: Jesus rursum sic eos alloquitur: O nati, quam difficile est fretos pecuniis in Dei regnum ingredi!"

Liberal Translation.

Matth. XXVII. 61.
Mary Magdalene and the other Mary, sitting on a place opposite the sepulchre, were *pleased spectators of these funeral obsequies.*

Mark X. 24.
Jesus resuming his discourse said, My dear companions, how extremely is it difficult for those who are *inflated* with their superior wealth, and *make it their great confidence and idol*, to enter into the Gospel-kingdom!

Dr. Harwood frequently explains words of the most easy interpretation by others more difficult to be understood. Had he constantly kept in view the pattern he professes to follow, he would not so often have done this.

Mark XV. 28.
And he was numbered with his transgressors.—Castalio: " Et inter sceleratos habitus est."

Mark XVI. 2.
And very early in the morning, the first day of the week, they came unto the sepulchre, at the rising of the sun.—Castalio: " Valde mane prima post sabbatum die veniunt ad monimentum orto jam sole."

Mark XV. 28.
He made *his exit*, confounded with the wicked.

Mark XVI. 2.
And very early on the first day of the week, they set out in a body for the sepulchre,—*the rays of the sun now streaking the edge of the horizon.*

It is somewhat curious to see the ornaments of diction lavished upon these plain words " ανατειλαντος τε ηλιε."

Luke I. 14.
And thou shalt have joy and gladness, and many shall rejoyce at his birth.—Castalio: " Qui tibi gaudio erit et laeti-

Luke I. 14.
His birth will not fill thy bosom only with the *purest transports*, but the *public* also will share in thine *extatic raptures.*

tix,

| *Present Version.* | *Liberal Translation.* |

tiæ, multique ex ejus nativitate gaudebunt."

Luke II. 13, 14.	Luke II. 13, 14.
And suddenly there was with the angel a multitude of the heavenly host praising God, and saying, Glory to God in the highest, and on earth peace, good will towards men. — Castalio: " Et repente extitit cum angelo cœlestium copiarum multitudo, Deum laudantium, et ita dicentium: Gloria in supremis Deo, et in terra pax, erga homines benevolentia."	The Angel ended — and was instantly joined by myriads of cœlestial spirits, who celebrated the divine benignity in the most sublime and rapturous strains, repeating, O let the highest angelic orders hymn the praise of God! O what happiness hath now blessed the world! O what ineffable benevolence is now expressed towards men!

The noble simplicity of this short hymn is totally enervated by an ill-judged show of eloquence.

John I. 36.	John I. 36.
Behold the Lamb of God. — Castalio: " Ecce agnus Dei."	Behold the amiable favourite of heaven.

What could tempt Dr. Harwood to wander from the literal rendering of this *emphatical* text, and to substitute in its place such flat and insipid expressions, it is difficult to conjecture.

Acts IX. 3.	Acts IX. 3.
And as he journeyed he came near Damascus; and suddenly there shined round about him a light from heaven.	And when he was now advanced within a little distance from Damascus, all on a sudden *a flood of light from the sky poured its effulgent splendors* around him.

There is nothing turgid in our present Version, or in Castalio: " Circumfulsit de cœlo lux."

Acts XIII. 47.	Acts XIII. 47.
For so hath the Lord commanded us, saying, I have set thee to be a light of the Gentiles, that thou shouldest be for salvation unto the ends of the earth.	For so hath God expressly enjoyned us to do by the prophet, I have appointed thee *to illuminate the dark and benighted Heathens with thy beams*, and to diffuse salvation and happiness to the extremity of the globe.

" Te gentibus externis lumen destinavi, ut sis ad ultimas usque terras saluti." Castalio. — Had Castalio written in English, his language would, I believe, have been equally *pure* and *elegant*, though certainly not so *diffusive*, as that of Dr. Harwood.

It is needless to trouble the reader with any more instances, as those which have been adduced are sufficient to convince him of the defects in the Liberal Translation. I should be sorry, however, to be thought willing to detract from the general merit of the author, from having been obliged by the nature of my subject to animadvert on this particular part of his works. The truth is, he undertook with a very good intention what was impracticable. The politest and most accurate Scholar, and the ablest Divine would have failed in the attempt. We must not therefore judge of Dr. Harwood from the imperfections of this work, but from his other writings, which have greatly contributed to promote the knowledge both of Sacred and Classical literature.

But to return to the point whence I have digressed. — I mentioned above, that a Version of the Scriptures should be as literal, as the genius of the English tongue will allow. Every language has many idioms peculiar to itself; and nothing is more absurd, than to torture our own, or any modern language whatever, in order to accommodate it to the Greek, or to the Hebrew. There are three exceptions to a literal translation, which naturally offer themselves; and which I shall touch upon only at present, as it is my design to illustrate them by a few examples in separate chapters.

I. *When*

I. *When the Language will not admit of a literal Translation, so as to make the Words sufficiently intelligible.*

One may presume, that this will be easily granted; for as it is the duty of a translator to impress us with the same ideas, which were intended to be given the reader by the author from whom he translated, it necessarily follows, that he ought to depart from the Greek text, when he cannot otherwise preserve the sense of it. This is so far from betraying a want of fidelity, that it is the only mean which can be employed to make the text clear and unequivocal. Father Simon affirms, that we ought to give professedly an ambiguous rendering of a Scriptural expression, when Divines are not agreed about the precise meaning of it*. An excellent mode of interpretation truly! as if a translator should conform himself to the passions or prejudices of any set of Divines. Let us compare this groundless and rash assertion with the opinion of a writer of the same communion, not more distinguished by his abilities, than by his liberality of sentiment: " Unwedded to systems of any kind, literary, physical, or religious, a translator of the Bible should sit down to render his author with the same indifference, he would sit down to render Thucydides or Xenophon. He should try to forget, that he belongs to any particular society of Christians; regardless of pleasing or displeasing any party †."

---

* See the preface to his Version of the New Testament.
† Prospectus of Dr. Geddes, p. 141.

II. *When the Times of Verbs will not admit of a literal Translation.*

It is well known, that the Tenses in the Original are frequently out of the regular and common order. We find both Past and Present Time used instead of the Future, that the certainty of an event may be more strongly marked. Nor will this appear extraordinary, if we consider, that the writers of the New Testament imitated the style and manner of the Seventy, who naturally incorporated the idioms of their mother-tongue into the Greek language. But to make this seeming confusion of Tenses intelligible to the common people, or even to any persons unacquainted with the Greek tongue, through the medium of a close verbal translation, is a point of the utmost difficulty. Perhaps the following distinction should be observed. When a Version is intended for the private use of readers, or for the learned only, a translator may with great propriety render literally the Tenses, as they stand in the Sacred writings; but when it is designed for the public service of the Church, and of course for general instruction, he should render them in a free manner, consistently with the nature of our language, to prevent the possibility of their being misunderstood.

III. *When Hebraisms and Græcisms are either redundant, or repugnant to the English idioms.*

That there are many redundant words in the New Testament, will scarcely be denied: whole dissertations are written on the subject; and indeed no language is intirely without expletives. But

But surely it is a strange practice to introduce any foreign expletives into our Version; for it can hardly be done without injuring the sense of it, or sacrificing the propriety of the English tongue. A translator of a Heathen author omits them without incurring any censure; and why the same licence should not be extended to a translator of the Bible, I cannot possibly see.

Beside the pleonasms servilely copied from the Greek and from the Hebrew, there are many stiff and barbarous expressions in our Present Version, derived from the same source. If marginal renderings be at all necessary, let them retain those expressions; but let nothing be admitted into the text, which we cannot read with pleasure, as well as with advantage.

CHAPTER X.

First Exception to a literal Translation, when the Language will not admit of it, so as to make the meaning of the Words sufficiently intelligible.

"AND Jesus went about all Galilee, teaching in their syna- Matth. IV. gogues, and preaching *the gospel of the kingdom* [good 23. tidings concerning the kingdom of God, or, of heaven."] The words in our Version carry with them no meaning at all; and it is to be wondered at, that ευαγγελιον was not rendered here by its primitive signification, which is much better adapted to this place.

Castalio

Caftalio has tranflated το ευαγγελιον της βασιλειας; "Evangelium regium," than which nothing can be more obfcure, according to Beza; but obfcure as it is, it does not feem to be more fo than "Evangelium regni," which is the rendering both by Beza, and the author of the Vulgate. A fimilar correction fhould take place in IX. 35. XXIV. 14. and likewife in XIII. 19. where ὁ λογος της βασιλειας ought to be tranflated " the doctrine concerning the kingdom of God, or, of heaven."— I cannot help obferving, by the way, that it would have done Beza credit, if he had retracted fome of the cenfures which he wantonly and unjuftly paffed upon Caftalio; for it cannot be denied, that Beza upon all occafions difcovered a fierce and vindictive difpofition, in infulting over the fuppofed miftakes, and in leffening the reputation of that accomplifhed fcholar.

Matth. X. 29.
" Are not two fparrows fold for a farthing? *and one of them fhall not fall* [yet not one of them falls] on the ground *without your Father* [without the permiffion, or, the will of your Father."] King James's tranflators undoubtedly thought they fhould be guilty of Heterodoxy, if they did not render literally ανευ τε πατρος ὑμων: not reflecting, that to fay, one does not fall on the ground without your Father, is the fame as to affirm, that *both* fall on it. Inaccurate as this is, we find it in all our old Englifh tranflations; and in all the Latin ones, which I have examined, except in that by Schmidius: " et tamen ne unicus ex illis cadit in terram fine *voluntate* Patris veftri," agreeably to which is the Verfion of Mons: " fans *la volonté* de voftre Pere," and the Verfion of L' Enfant and Beaufobre: " fans *la permiffion* de votre Pere," and alfo that of Diodati: " fenza '*l volere* del Padre voftro." Mr. Wakefield, to whom the admirers of Claffical elegance are highly indebted for

for his notes upon this Gospel, has fully explained this form of expression, ανευ τȣ πατρος ὑμων, and has shewn it to be not only a Hebraism, but common to the purest writers of Greece and Rome; yet he would not venture to transfer their idiom into the English language, but has judiciously rendered it "without *the will of your Father*."— The ingenious author of "an essay for a new translation of the Bible" proposes to render ασσαριον " a penny," because it was a Syrian coin of that value; but it is far from being certain, that St. Matthew alludes to it; however, I cannot forbear taking the opportunity to remark, that this anonymous writer has pointed out several mistakes of our Translators, in expressing the coins, weights, and measures mentioned in Holy writ *.

"For whosoever *hath* [hath much] to him shall be given, and he shall have more abundance; but whosoever *hath not* [hath little] from him shall be taken away even *that* [what] he hath." If men of letters can comprehend, how any thing can be taken away from a man who has nothing, it must doubtless be unintelligible to the common people. — Matth. XIII. 12.

"Wo unto you, ye blind guides, *which* [who] say, Whosoever shall swear *by* [only by] the temple, it is nothing; but whosoever shall swear by the gold of the temple, *he is a debter* [is bound by his oath."] This seems to be the best interpretation of οφειλει, and leaves no room for ambiguity. So ver. 18. "And whosoever shall swear *by* [only by] the altar, it is nothing; but whosoever sweareth by the gift that is upon it, *he is guilty* [is bound by his oath." Il faut qu'il tient son ferment, as L'Enfant and Beausobre — XXIII. 16.

* The second edition of this essay, which is by far the most complete, was published 1727.

sobre interpret it. One cannot help observing, that king James's translators have rendered εσυλα differently in these two verses, though it evidently has the same meaning in both; a fault, which is not to be met with in any Versions, except the English. Bishop Newcome remarks, that when an English word suits every place, it should be invariably used; and that our Translators often vary their terms not only unnecessarily, but so as to mislead the reader. His Lordship has referred us, among other instances, to John II. 9. where the same person is called in the same verse, both the ruler and governour of the feast*. A notable example in this kind occurs in Acts XVII. 19. " And they took him, and brought him unto *Areopagus* [the court of Areopagus.] (22) Then Paul *stood in the midst of Mars-hill* [stood *up* in the midst of *the court of Areopagus.*"] Had our Translators intended to puzzle the middle and lower ranks of people, a more effectual method could not have been taken; it being impossible for them to know, that Areopagus and Mars-hill denote the same place. But it seems, that our Translators were a little upon their guard; for they have inserted Mars-hill in the margin opposite to Areopagus; and Areopagus in the margin opposite to Mars-hill; that such as have an opportunity or inclination to consult their notes, may be secure from error; but this idle parade of learning would have been needless, if they had followed Tyndal and the bulk of the English translators in rendering Αρειος παγος in both verses after the same manner.—I shall mention another instance in Acts VIII. St. Luke speaking of Simon Magus from ver. 9. to ver. 13. uses εξιςων, εξιςηκεναι, and εξιςατο, which manifestly have the same meaning. The Vulgate, however, has rendered them by *seducens*,

demen-

---

* Preface to the Version of the minor Prophets, p. xxvii.

(127)

dementaffet, and *stupens admirabatur*, which hath occasioned a heavy censure from Laurentius Valla. King James's translators have not gone so far as the Vulgate; but they have servilely copied after the Bishops-Bible, in rendering them two different ways, namely, *wondered*, and *bewitched*; and though they may not deserve to be so severely handled as the author of the Vulgate, yet we cannot but acknowledge, that they have been very unfortunate in their choice of the Verb *bewitched*.

"And he said unto them, Unto you it is given to know the mystery of the kingdom of God; but to them *that* [who] are without, all these things *are done* [are] in parables." Whether we ought with Dr. Lightfoot to render οἱ ἔξω "the Gentiles;" or with Dr. Clarke "the mixt multitude;" or with Bengelius "extra discipulatum genuinum," or to follow other interpreters, I do not take upon me to determine; but it is evident, that the word *without* can convey no satisfactory idea to an English reader; or perhaps no idea at all. I have followed Bishop Pearce in rendering ε. παραβολαις τα παντα γινεται "all things are in parables," that is, spoken in them; but I cannot possibly agree with his Lordship in applying οἱ ἔξω to those only, whom Jesus had taught on the sea-shore; and who were not then in the house with him, when he spake in private to the Twelve.

Mark IV. 11.

"And he *could do there no* mighty works, *save* [except] that he *laid* [put] his hands on a few sick *folk* [persons] and healed them." Ουκ εδυνατο has been thus almost universally rendered; and has given occasion to numberless comments and notes; all which might have been spared, if it had been rendered "did not judge proper to do," or "was not willing to do," in which latter sense

— VI. 5.

it

it is used by the LXX according to Mintert, who explains it by "voluit, desideravit."

Mark XI. 25.
" And when ye *stand praying*, forgive, if ye have *aught* against any &c." The rule of forgiveness extends certainly to all mankind, whether they pray standing, or kneeling, or in any other attitude; but our Translators, by rendering ςηκετε according to its primitive meaning, confine this rule in some measure to such as *pray standing*. I am far from insinuating, that this was the intention of our Translators, or that the sense of the passage is very likely to be misunderstood; but it is clear, that the word *standing* seems to imply it, which is a sufficient reason why it ought to be corrected. It had better have been " And when ye shall *dispose*, or *prepare* yourselves for praying, if ye have any matter of complaint against any person, forgive him &c." We see in Mintert, that ιςημι is used by the LXX to express " ratus sum, paratus sum, dispono." L'Enfant and Beausobre have taken it in the last sense: " Mais quand vous vous disposerez à prier." —It will not be amiss to observe here, that the Verb ιςημι has led our Translators into frequent errors. Mr. Markland observes, " that all Verbs of *posture*, or *gesture*, as *to go, to walk, to stand, to sit* &c. in good Greek writers (and some in Latin) have the signification of *existere, to be* *." This remark is undoubtedly well-grounded; and yet it is the general practice of our Translators to render ιςημι literally, " I stand," even when the context cannot possibly admit of it. Thus it is said in Acts IX. 7. that the men who journeyed with St. Paul *stood* speechless, though St. Paul affirms,

* Bowyer's Critical Conjectures &c. p. 25.—and see Wakefield's note on Matthew VI. 5.

affirms, that he himself and his companions fell to the earth; and, what is surprizing, Mr. Wynne also has rendered ἐξεπλάγησαν "stood amazed."—It is said John I. 35. "Again the next day after, John *stood*, and two of his disciples." Can we imagine, that the Evangelist intended to describe the posture of the Baptist? It ought to be "John *was* again there, with two of his disciples." Thus Castalio: "Postridie rursus *aderat* Johannes," and likewise the Version of Mons: "Le lendemain Jean *estoit* encore là avec deux de ses disciples." Diodati has rendered it somewhat differently, but much better than in our translation: "Il giorno seguente, Giovanni di nuovo *si fermò* con due de' suoi discepoli." —There is another Verb, viz. πορευομαι, which ought not always to be rendered literally. Thus Luke XIII. 33. "Nevertheless *I must walk* to day, and to morrow, and the day following." It should be "I must continue my course or preaching &c." It seems a proverbial manner of describing an event which would soon happen, as Bishop Newcome has remarked upon Hosea VI. 2. where we meet with a phrase in this kind.

"As it is written in the law of the Lord, *Every male that openeth the womb* [every first-born male child] shall be *called holy* [consecrated] to the Lord." This is rather more decent, and equally expressive, though not literal. Thus Beza: omnis masculus primogenitus," and Schmidius: "omne masculinum primogenitum," and the Version of Mons, "tout enfant masle premier né sera consacré au Seigneur." Luke II. 23.

"Saying, Master, *Moses wrote unto us*, If any man's brother die, having a wife &c." Had the words Μωσης εγραψεν ἡμιν been rendered thus: "Moses left us this command in writing," the meaning of the passage would have been obvious; but an ill- —XX. 28.

judged

judged adherence to the text is likely to prevent illiterate perſons from underſtanding it. The French Verſions are much the cleareſt in the tranſlation of this verſe. That of Mons hath " Moyſe nous a laiſſé cette ordonannce par écrit," and that of L' Enfant and Beauſobre " Moïſe nous a laiſſé par écrit."

Luke XXII. 2.
" And the chief prieſts and ſcribes *ſought how they might kill him*, for they feared the multitude." In the firſt place, the Pronoun *him* is in the ſecond verſe of a chapter without an Antecedent; and, ſecondly, the words import, that the reaſon why they determined to kill Jeſus, was, becauſe they feared the people; which cannot but appear to be a very extraordinary reaſon. All will be right, if we make a very little addition, and render it " ſought a *convenient* opportunity to put *Jeſus* to death." Thus Schmidius: " et quærebant quomodo *commodé* eum de medio tollerent." It is rendered in the Vulgate " timebant *vero* plebem," which makes it probable, that the Vulgate followed another reading, viz. εϕοβυντο δε τον λαον, not γαρ, and this reading is ſupported by the Cambridge MS. and makes any addition unneceſſary. The Spaniſh Verſion has preferred it; " Y los principes de los ſacerdotes y los eſcribas procuravan como lo matarian; *mas* avian miedo del pueblo." And Wicklif and Tyndal have likewiſe preferred it.

John III. 33.
" He *that* [who] hath received his teſtimony, *hath ſet to his ſeal* [hath confirmed as it were by his ſeal] that God is true." Εσϕραγισεν ſhould be rendered thus VI. 27. Eraſmus ſays, " hoc eſt, ſigno confirmavit; nam ſigillum additum rem certam efficit." The literal tranſlation is very harſh. Wicklif has not mentioned the ſeal at all: " But he that takith his witneſſing, hath *confermed* that God is ſoithfaſt."

— V. 70.
" Jeſus anſwered them, Have not I choſen you twelve, *and*
[and

[and yet] one of you is *a devil* [a traitor, or falfe accufer."] The Particle και here fignifies " and yet," as in many places in the N. T. Tyndal has rendered it fo in this verfe: " Have not I chofen you twelve, *and yet* one of you is *the* devyl?" but it is a little furprizing, that he fhould ufe here the Definite Article.

" The number of the *names* [perfons] together *were* [was] about an hundred and twenty." Οχλος ονοματων is rendered literally in the Vulgate, and in fome of our Englifh Verfions; but it is not fo in Wicklif: " And there was a cumpanye of men togidre almeft an hundride and twenti." Nor in the Rhemifh N. T. " the multitude of perfons." Acts I. 15.

" Wherefore *of thefe men which have companied with us* [one of thefe men who have accompanied us] all the time that the Lord Jefus *went in and out* among us." The Vulgate hath " intravit et exivit," but Beza contends, that the Hebraifm εισηλθε και εξηλθεν is very obfcure, when tranflated literally; and therefore he renders it, " verfatus eft." The Zurich Verfion hath " toto tempore quo Dominus Jefus munere fuo functus eft inter nos." It is in Cranmer's Bible " had all his converfation among us," and in Tomfon's, and the Geneva Bible, " converfant among us." It is rather ftrange that king James's tranflators difregarded the latter rendering, which at this day could not be done with more propriety—So Acts IX. 28. εισπορευομενος και εκπορευομενος μετ' αυτων fhould be rendered after the fame manner. — 21.

" And the Lord added to the church daily *fuch as fhould be faved* [Chriftian converts, or converts to Chriftianity."] This feems to be the true meaning of τυς σωζομενυς, and perhaps it would be as well to render εκλεκτυς, and words of a fimilar fignification, in the like manner. For the beft explanation of thefe terms, fee the

the VIth chapter of that imcomparable book, "The key to the Apostolic writings."

Acts VI. 2. "Then the twelve called *the multitude of the disciples unto them* [all the disciples together] and said, It is not *reason* [reasonable] that we should leave the word of God, *and serve tables* [and attend upon the tables *of the poor*."]

—IX. 2. "And desired of him letters *to Damascus to the synagogues* [to the synagogues at Damascus,] that if he *found* [should find] any of this *way* [sect] whether they were men or women, he might bring them bound to Jerusalem." Tremellius has strangely mistaken the sense of της οδου οντας, which he renders, "ut si ita esset ut inveniret qui iter facerent *per hanc viam*," but our Translators are likely to lead many readers into the same error; and I cannot conceive, why they rendered ὁδος in ver. 2. after the same manner as in ver. 27. where it is used according to its primary signification. 'οδος in ver. 2. is the same with αιρεσις in XXVIII. 22. "But we desire to hear *of thee* [from thee] what thou thinkest; for as *concerning* [to] this sect, we know that every where it is spoken against." Beza, and Schmidius use the word *secta* in ver. 2. and to the same purport are the French and Italian Versions; and even the Spanish one, which does not often deviate from the letter, says "*de esta secta*."—It will not be amiss to take notice of two or three passages in the Acts, where ὁδος is ill translated. Thus XIX. 9. "But when *divers* [many] were hardened, and believed not, but spake *evil* [contemptuously] of *that way* before the multitude, he departed from them &c." It should be "that religion," or, "the doctrine of the Lord," as it is rendered by L'Enfant and Beausobre: "la doctrine du Seigneur." Again, ver. 23. "And the same time there arose no small *stir about that way*

way [tumult on account of that religion."] — Again, XXII. 4. " And I perfecuted *this way unto the death* [the followers of this religion unto death."] Bifhop Lowth has juftly obferved, that the Definite Article is here improperly ufed, becaufe the Apoftle does not mean any particular fort of death, but death in general*: it furprized me, however, that his Lordfhip paffed by unnoticed the reft of the verfe, which ftood equally in need of his correction. — I have rendered ὁδος differently in the above-mentioned verfes, notwithftanding what I have advanced about an uniformity of rendering; but the reafon is apparent: ὁδος is one of thofe words which will not always admit of being tranflated in the fame manner. It may be called a *fect*, when fpoken of by the unbelieving Jews; but cannot be juftly called fo, when fpoken of by the Apoftles, becaufe it is now become, though perhaps improperly, a term of reproach.

" And they faid, Cornelius, the centurion, a juft man, *and one that feareth God* [and a profelyte] and of good report among all the nation of the Jews, was warned from God by an holy angel, to fend for thee, *and to hear the words of thee*." Και ακυται ρηματα παρα σε. It would be better " to hear, or receive thy inftructions," or, " to hear *thy* words," as it is in the Geneva Bible. So XI. 14. " Who fhall *tell thee words*, whereby thou and all thy houfe fhall be faved." It would be better " give thee inftructions, or, inftruct thee in doctrines." Diodati has judicioufly rendered it " il quale ti ragionerà delle cofe." Acts X. 22.

" For they heard them *fpeak with tongues*, and magnified God." ── ── 46. Λαλειν γλωσσαις doubtlefs ought not to be rendered literally. It is certain, that the Gentiles " fpake with tongues" before they received

* Introduction to Englifh grammar, p. 16.

ceived the gift of the Holy Ghost; and it could be no cause of astonishment to the Jews, that they did so afterward. To make it intelligible to the common people, we ought to translate it " For they heard them speak in *different* languages." So Mark XVI. 17. " they shall speak *with new tongues* [in different languages."] Thus likewise Acts II. 4. " *and began to speak with other tongues* [and spake in different languages."] It is well known, that *tongue* is often used indiscriminately for *language*; but, in this sense, it will not bear to be governed by the Preposition *with*. However, if *defendit numerus* be a sufficient apology for sacrificing sense to words, king James's translators are abundantly justified; there being scarce any exceptions to this strange mode of rendering, but in the French and Italian Versions.

Acts XI. 22.   " Then tidings of these things came *unto the ears of the church* which was in Jerusalem, and they sent forth Barnabas &c." It would be better thus: " When the report of these things had come to the knowledge of the church which was in Jerusalem, they sent forth Barnabas &c." A literal translation of εις τα ωτα is very harsh. Schmidius has done it in another manner, but still more uncouth if possible. " Auditus est autem hic rumor de illis, *arcana auditione* Ecclesiæ."

—— — 23.   " Who, when he *came* [arrived there] and *had seen the grace* [saw the gracious dispensation] of God, was glad, and exhorted *them all, that with purpose of heart they would cleave unto the Lord* [all of them to adhere resolutely unto the Lord."] Surely this Adverb expresses much better the meaning of προθεσει της καρδιας, than either " purpose of heart," or, proposito cordis," which is the verbal rendering by the Vulgate, and by Beza. Tremellius has more properly translated it " toto corde adhærerent."

" Men

"*Men and brethren, children* [Brethren, ye who are children] of the stock of Abraham, *and whosoever among you feareth God* [and ye who are proselytes] to you is the word of this salvation sent." Though φοβεμενος τον Θεον, and σεβομενος τον Θεον, expressions which so often occur in the Acts, are universally allowed to mean *proselytes*, yet few translators have had the courage to depart from the letter of the text. " Qui timet Deum," or, " qui colit Deum," and words of the like import, may be equally applied to a religious Pagan. It is curious enough to see the barbarism of the Vulgate in the verse above-mentioned: " Viri fratres, filii generis Abraham, et *qui in vobis timent* Deum."

Acts XIII. 26.

" For they *that* [who] dwell at Jerusalem, and their rulers, because they *knew him not* [knew not *Jesus*] nor yet the *voices* [writings] of the prophets, which are read every sabbath-day &c." To read *voices*, is a little extraordinary. If our Translators did not choose to render φωναι " writings" they should at least have rendered it " the words," as it is in Tomson's, and in the Geneva Bible. It is the same in L'Enfant and Beausobre: " les paroles des prophetes."

— — 27.

" Then the priest of Jupiter *which was before their city* [whose statue, or, whose temple was before their city] brought oxen and garlands unto the gates, and would have *done* [offered] sacrifice with the people." Ζευς — προ της πολεως is like Οικα προ πολεως in Æschylus, as Mr. Markland observes; they both denote either a temple, or a statue before the city; but though it is good Greek, a literal translation into English, or indeed into most languages, will not convey the same meaning. Schmidius has supplied the ellipsis: " Sacerdos autem Jovis, *cujus idolum* collocatum erat ante urbem eorum." The same is done by the author of the Version

— XIV. 13.

of

of Mons: "Et même le facrificateur *(du temple)* de Jupiter, qui étoit près de la ville," and likewife by L'Enfant and Beaufobre: "Même le Prêtre de Jupiter, dont *le temple* étoit devant la ville." So Diodati: "E l'facerdote di Jove, il cui *tempio* era davanti alla lor città." It may perhaps be queftioned, whether our early Englifh tranflators underftood the meaning of this verfe. Tyndal has rendered it thus: "Then Jupiter's priefte, *whych dwelte* before the cytye, brought oxen and garlands unto the churche porche &c." and in much the fame manner we find it rendered by Coverdale, Cranmer, Mathew, and Taverner. There is fome reafon alfo to fufpect, that king James's tranflators mifunderftood the fenfe of this paffage.

Acts XXI. 21.
"And they are informed *of* [concerning] thee, that thou teacheft all the Jews *which* [who] are among the Gentiles, to forfake Mofes, faying, that they ought not to circumcife their children, *neither* [nor] to *walk after the cuftoms.*" It may be taken for granted, that the Jews and primitive Chriftians comprehended the meaning of ἔθεα, when fimply ufed by itfelf; juft as the fignification of the word *Statutes* is well known among us; but how is it poffible for our common people to form an idea of the phrafe "*to walk after the cuftoms?*" It ought to be "the cuftoms of our fathers," or, "the cuftoms, or rites eftablifhed by Mofes," or fomething in this kind. Among the various readings in Curcellæus's Teftament, ἔθεσι τοις πατρῴοις is mentioned; and in Stephens's edition of 1550 (which king James's tranflators are faid chiefly to have ufed) τοις πατρῴοις is put in the magin; and one of Stephens's MSS. is cited as authority for it. Thefe tranflators had probably fome reafon for rejecting this reading; but ftill they ought to have made an addition by way of fupplement, that the
fentence

sentence might be intelligible. This is done by Schmidius: "secundum ritus *Mosis* ambulent," and by Tremellius: "in ritibus *Legis*," and by the author of the Version of Mons: "selon les coutumes *reçues parmi les Juifs*."

"And desired favour *against him*, that he would send for *him* [Paul] to Jerusalem, *laying wait in the way to kill him*." It should be "intending to lie in wait upon the road to kill him," as it is observed by Bishop Pearce and Mr. Markland; for it appears, that the reason of their application to Festus to send for Paul to Jerusalem, was that they might have an opportunity to murder Paul upon the road; but they did not actually lie in wait, as our Version intimates, when they applied to Festus. Our Translators did not consider, that ενεδραν ποιευντες was used here for ενεδραν ποιησοντες, and that therefore it was not to be rendered literally.— The expression "desired favour *against him*" is as uncouth as possible; and yet we find it generally adopted. There are a few MSS. which have not κατ' αυτυ, but παρ' αυτυ, greatly, in my opinion, to be preferred. It would then run thus: "and requested it as a favour *from* him." Tremellius has chosen this reading: "Et petierunt *ab eo* (rogantes eum) hanc gratiam &c." So it is in the Version of Mons: "Ils *luy demandoient* comme une grace, qu' il le fist venir à Jerusalem," and in L'Enfant and Beausobre: "Ils *le prièrent* de leur accorder cette grace."

Act XXV. 3.

"For there stood by me this night *the* [an] angel *of God* [of the God] whose I am, and whom I serve, (24) Saying, Fear not, Paul, thou must be brought before Cæsar: and lo! God *hath given thee* [hath for thy sake preserved] all them *that* [who] sail with thee." Doth it not seem necessary to use some little periphrasis, when so very few readers can understand the meaning

—XXVII. 23.

of κεχαρισαι tranflated literally?—In the 23d verfe I have rendered αγγελος; *an* angel, not *the* angel; an alteration, which is required in many places in the N. T. as it has been often remarked. But the moft ftriking inftance in this kind is in the IId chapter of St. Matthew. It is faid in the 13th verfe, that " *the* angel of God appeareth to Jofeph," and in the 19th, that " *an* angel of God appeareth to Jofeph." We fhould be tempted to imagine, that this chapter was rendered by different perfons, if it did not appear, that king James's tranflators fometimes confound the two Articles in the very fame verfe.

CHAPTER XI.

Second Exception to a literal Tranflation, when the Times of Verbs will not admit of it.

Matth. II. 9. "WHEN they had heard the king, they departed; and lo! the ftar *which they faw* in the Eaft, went before them, till it came and ftood *over* [over the place] where the young child was." It fhould be " which they had feen," as in the Geneva Bible; that is, " which they had at firft feen in the Eaft." Ειδον is properly rendered by " viderant" in almoft all the Latin Verfions; and after the fame manner in the French, Spanifh, and Italian.

—. VIII. 33. " And they *that* [who] kept them, fled, *and went their ways* [and went] into the city, and told *every thing* [all thefe things] and

and what *was befallen to the possessed of the devils* [had befallen the demoniacs." It is right in Tyndal: "and what *had* fortuned unto &c." and also in Coverdale, and Cranmer.

"Then *began he* [he began] to upbraid the cities wherein most of his mighty works *were done* [had been done,] because they repented not." Beza has rendered ἐγένοντο by *editæ fuerant*. So Diodati: "Nelle quali la maggior parte delle sue potenti operazioni *erano state*," and the author of the Spanish Version: "en las quales *avian sido* hechas muy muchas de sus maravillas," and thus too the Version of Mons: "dans lesquelles il *avoit fait* plusieurs miracles." Our Translators have committed the same fault in the 21ſt verse. Matth. XI. 20.

"Then Jesus called his disciples unto him, and said, I have compassion on the multitude, *because they continue with me three days.*" It should be "because they *have* continued with me three days," as in the Geneva Bible, and in most of our old Versions. The words in the Original, ὅτι ἤδη ἡμέρας τρεῖς προσμένουσί μοι, occur in Mark VIII. 2. where they are justly rendered "because they *have* now *been* with me three days." Instances in this kind are so frequent, that we are naturally led to suspect, that king James's translators were not guided by any consistent and uniform rule. — XV. 32.

"Behold! your house is *left* unto you desolate." Rather "shall be left," as in Wicklif, and in almost all our Versions, except the Bishops-Bible. So L'Enfant and Beausobre: "Sachez donc que votre demeure *va devenir* deserte." Though ἀφίεται is the word in the Original, it is rendered in the Vulgate by *relinquetur*, which is injudiciously changed into *relinquitur* by Beza. — XXIII. 38.

"Watch therefore; for ye know not *what hour* [at what hour] your Lord *doth come* [is to come, or, will come.]" Ἔρχεται is rendered —. XXIV. 42.

dered "venturus fit" by the author of the Vulgate, and by Beza, and in the Zurich Verfion; and it is rendered in Future Time by almoſt all our old tranſlators. Thus Wicklif: "Therefore wake ye, for ye witen not in what our the Lord ſchal come." So Tyndal: "wil come;" and there is hardly an exception to it, but in the Biſhops-Bible. There are many fimilar paſſages in the N. T. which require the fame correction.

Matth. XXVI. 2.

"Ye know that after two days *is* [will be] the feaſt of the paſſover, and the Son of man *is* [will be] betrayed to be crucified." Here again king James's tranſlators followed the Biſhops-Bible. It is not fo in Wicklif: "Ye witen that aftir tweyn dayes Paſke *ſchal be* maad, and mannes fone *ſchal be* bitakun to be crucified." Nor in Tyndal, Coverdale, and Cranmer; nor in the Rhemiſh Verfion, in which it is thus tranſlated: "You know that after two dayes *ſhal be* Pafche, and the Son of man *ſhal be* delivered to be crucified." Γινεται and παραδιδοται are rendered in Future Time by the Vulgate: "Scitis quia poſt biduum Paſcha *fiet*, et Filius hominis *tradetur* ut crucifigatur;" and in the like manner by Beza, Caſtalio, and Schmidius. The tranſlation in Tomſon's, and in the Geneva Bible differs from all: "Ye know that after two days *is* the paſſover, and the Son of man *ſhall be* delivered to be crucified." This unqueſtionably is very inaccurate; for the two Verbs ought to have been rendered in the fame Time.

—— — 24.

"The Son of man *goeth* [is going out of the world, or, is about to die] as it is written of him; but wo unto that man by whom the Son of man *is betrayed* [ſhall be betrayed."] Mr. Markland obſerves upon John XVI. 4. that the Verb ὑπαγω "to go" (which is uſed in this verſe) is common to the beſt Greek, as well as the Sacred writers; and Alberti makes the following remark upon

upon the above-mentioned verse in St. Matthew: "ὑπάγει, moritur, perinde ac Lat. obire, abire, et perire. Sic διοίχεται pro moritur Menandri fragmentis." All this is true; yet it becomes bad English, and perhaps quite unintelligible to the common people, when it is translated literally.

"And they come to Jesus, and see him *that was possessed with*   Mark V. 15. *the devil* [who *had been* a demoniac &c.] (16) And they *that* [who] saw it told them, *how it befel to him that was possessed with the devil* [what had *befallen* him who *had been* a demoniac."] In the 18th verse, it is expressed after this manner; but the man was undoubtedly cured, when the people came to Jesus, as related in the 15th verse; for it is said, that the man was *in his right mind*; therefore the sense necessarily requires, that δαιμονιζομενος should be rendered in the Past Definite Time, as well as δαιμονισθεις. It is remarkably correct in the Spanish Version: (15) "alque *avia sido* atormentado del demonio," (16) "como avia acontecido alque *avia* tenido el demonio," (18) "el que *avia sido* fatigado del demonio." Few translators have been so exact in this instance as Cypriano de Valera.

"And immediately he talked with them, and *saith* [said] unto   —VI. 50. them, Be of good cheer, it is I, be not afraid." Our Translators have rendered literally ελαλησε and λεγει, as the Vulgate has done; but they had better have rendered them in the same Time "talked and said," as in the Geneva Bible, and in some other old Versions. This seems more agreeable to our own, as well as to almost every modern language. Thus Diodati: "egli tosto *parlò* con loro, e *disse*," and so likewise the author of the Spanish Version: "mas luego *habló* con ellos, y les *dixo*." But it is still better to use a Participle and a Verb, instead of two Verbs: Thus
Castalio:

Castalio: "Tum ille continuo eos *allocatus*, Bono este animo, *inquit*: ego sum, ne timete."

Mark XI. 24.
"Therefore I say unto you, what things soever ye desire when ye pray, believe that ye *receive them* [will receive them] and ye shall have them." It is rendered thus by Wicklif: "believe ye that ye *schulen* take, and thei *schulen* come to you," and after the same manner in the Geneva Bible: "believe that ye *shall* have it, and it shall be done unto you;" and we find the same in Tyndal, and in Coverdale, and in the French, Spanish, and Italian Versions. The Vulgate hath *accipietis*, and Beza *accepturos*. Though λαμβανετε may imply a certainty of the thing spoken of, yet that idea cannot be conveyed by the English Verb *receive*, unless it be rendered in Future Time.

—XV. 6.
"Now at that feast *he released* [he used to release] unto them one prisoner, whomsoever they desired." The Vulgate renders απελυεν by "solebat dimittere," which Beza turns into "dimittebat," though he says expressly in his notes, that απελυεν has the force of "absolvere et liberare solebat." Some of the English translators, as well as the Latin, follow the Vulgate. Thus Wicklif: "But by the feeste day *he was wont* to leeve to hem oon of men bounden whome ever thei axiden." So Tyndal: "At that feaste Pylate *was wont* to deliver at theyr pleasure a prisoner, whomsoever they woulde desyer." And we find the same in the Version of Mons: "Or il *avoit accoustumé* de delivrer à la feste de Pasque &c."

Luke XV. 29.
"And he answering said to his father, Lo! these many years do I *serve thee* [I have served thee.]" Not one of our antient Versions is faulty in this respect.

—XIX. 8.
"And Zaccheus *stood* [stood forth] and said unto the Lord, Behold!

hold! Lord, the half of my goods *I give* [I will give] unto the poor; and if I have taken any thing from any man by false accusation, *I restore* [I will restore] him four-fold." Verba sunt agnoscentis peccatum, as Vatablus says. Zaccheus seems determined to make ample restitution, as well as to be liberal in relieving the poor; but how will this appear, unless δίδωμι be rendered in Future Time? Of all the Versions which I have examined, that of Mons has the most accurately represented this passage: " Seigneur, *je m' en vais donner* la moitié de mon bien aux pauvres; & si j'ay fait tort à quelqu' un en quoy que ce soit, *je luy en rendray* quatre fois autant."

" And they drew nigh unto the village, whither *they went* [they were going] and he *made as though he would have gone further* [pretended that he was going farther."] — So John VI. 21. " Then they willingly received him into the *ship* [boat] and immediately the *ship* [boat] was at the land *whither they went*." It should be " whither they were going." There are other passages where our Translators have used improperly the Verb, instead of the Present Participle.

Luke XXIV. 28.

" And behold! *I send* [I will send] the promise of my Father upon you; but *tarry ye* [continue] in the city of Jerusalem, until ye be endued with power from on high." The latter part of the verse plainly shews, that the promise was not already completed. Αποστελλω is rendered by *mittam* almost universally in the Latin Versions; and indeed in most of the English ones. Thus Wicklif: " And I *schal* send the biheest of my Fadir into you." Thus also Tyndal: " And behold, I *wyll* send the promyses of my father upon you:" and in this instance the Bishops-Bible is exact. Αποστελλω is likewise rendered in Future Time in the Spanish Version:

— — 49.

sion: "Y heaqui *yo embiaré* al Prometido de mi Padre sobre vosotros:" and also in the Version of Mons: "*Et je m' en vais envoyer sur vous le don de mon Pere qui vous a esté promis.*" So too L' Enfant and Beausobre: "*Je vais vous envoyer* &c."

John IV. 46. "So Jesus came again into Cana of Galilee, where he *made the water wine* [*had* made the water wine, or rather, *had* changed the water into wine."] Επωιησεν is rightly translated in all the Versions which I have seen, except in the Vulgate, and in the English Bibles. St. John alludes to the miracle which had been wrought in Cana the first time that Jesus was there; but this does not appear from our translation; nor can it possibly appear, unless the Aorist be rendered in Past Definite Time.

——VI. 19. "So when they had rowed about five and twenty, or thirty furlongs, they *see* [saw] Jesus walking on the *sea* [lake] and drawing nigh unto the *ship* [boat] and they were afraid. The Verbs θεωρουσι and εφοβηθησαν are very properly rendered in the same Time in most of our Bibles; but this is not the case with the Vulgate: "conspiciunt et metuerunt," nor with Beza, who adopts the same words; nor with the Zurich Version: "vident et timuerunt." But Castalio is more accurate: "aspiciunt et territi sunt."—Thus John V. 14. "Afterward Jesus *findeth* him in the temple, and *said* unto him." Both Verbs ought undoubtedly to be either in Past, or in Present Time. Most of our old translators had too much judgement to render literally ευρισκει and ειπεν. We find in Wicklif "fond and seide;" in Taverner, "founde and seide;" and in many others "founde and sayde." Castalio has with great propriety used a Participle: "Postea nactus eum Jesus in fano, sic alloquitur &c."

—. VII. 33. "Then said Jesus unto them, *Yet a little while am I with you*
[But

[But little longer *shall I be* with you] and then *I go* [I shall go] unto him that [who] sent me." (34) "Ye shall seek me, and not find me: and where *I am* [I shall be] thither ye cannot come." So XII. 35. "Then Jesus said unto them, *Yet a little while is* [But little longer *will be*] the light with you &c." So again XIII. 33. "Little children, *yet a little while I am with you* [but little longer *shall I be* with you.] Ye shall seek me: and, as I said unto the Jews, whither *I go* [I am going] ye cannot come; so now I say unto you." We may observe here, that the expressions ετι μικρον χρονον, and ετι μικρον are common to the LXX. Thus Hosea I. 4. διοτι οτι μικρον, και εκδικησω το αιμα &c. and after the same manner Jonah III. 4. ετι τρεις ημεραι, και Νινευη καταςραφησεται.

"Then again called they the man *that was blind*." It should be "who had been blind:" for he had recovered his sight at the time they called him. 'Ος εν τυφλος is rendered "qui fuerat cæcus" in almost all the Latin Versions; and "that had been blind" in Tomson's, and in the Geneva Bible.   John IX. 24.

"*Jesus knowing* [Though Jesus knew] that the Father had given all things into his hands, and that *he was come from God, and went to God* [he came from God, and was returning to God."] In all our antient Versions we meet with the same ungrammatical translation of ὑπαγει.   —. XIII. 3.

"*Now Caiaphas was he which gave counsel to the Jews* [Now it was Caiaphas who *had given* counsel to the Jews] that it was expedient that one man should die for the people." St. John evidently refers to the advice of Caiaphas mentioned XI. 50. before Jesus was apprehended; but this will not appear, if συμβυλευσας be not rendered by the Past Definite. We find *confilium dederant* in the Vulgate, and in Beza; and the three foreign Versions in   —. XVIII. 14.

modern languages, so frequently appealed to, are very exact: in the Italian " ch' avea consigliato," — in the Spanish : " el que avia dado el consejo," — and in the Version of Mons " qui avoit donné ce conseil." Of all the old English Bibles, which I have examined, the Rhemish alone has been accurate in this particular: " And Caiaphas was he that *had given* the counsel to the Jews, that it is expedient, that one man die for the people."

John XX. 6. " Then *cometh* Simon Peter following him, and *went* into the sepulchre, and *seeth* the linen clothes *lie* [lying."] Here a Perfect Tense is slipt in between two Present Tenses after a very extraordinary manner. It is thus indeed in the Original: — ερχεται — εισηλθεν — θεωρει. But will any one contend, that it makes good English, because it makes good Greek? Either it ought to be " goeth into the sepulchre," or, there should be used three Verbs in Past Time, as in the Vulgate: — venit — introivit — vidit — and as, in fact, it is in our antient translations, and in the French, Spanish, and Italian Versions.

Acts III. 10. " And they knew that it was he *which sat* [who had sitten, or, who used to sit] at the Beautiful gate of the temple." St. Luke says, that the lame man, who had been healed, was actually in the temple, when the people saw him; but if ην καθημενος be not rendered by a word of Past Definite Time, he might possibly be sitting then at the gate. It is to no purpose to say, that the sense is not likely to be misapprehended; for, as it has been often above intimated, there is no excuse for ambiguous expressions. The Version of Mons, which is for the most part very accurate in respect to Tenses, has rendered it " celui là même qui *avoit accôutumé* d'estre à la Belle porte &c." which is the same with *solitus sedere* in Castalio. The author of the Vulgate, and Beza, like

our

our Translators, have rendered it by *sedebat*. Had they said, "sedebat quotidie," as Tremellius has done, it would have been right.

"*Howbeit many of them which heard the word believed* [Yet many of those who *had heard* the discourse believed.*"*] Both the Vulgate, and Beza use *audierant*; and indeed it is rendered properly by all, unless by Tremellius, and the early English translators. We must, however, except Wicklif the father of them: " but manye of hem that *hadden herd* the word bileevyden."

Acts IV. 4.

CHAPTER XII.

Third Exception to a literal Translation, when Hebraisms or Græcisms are either redundant or repugnant to the English Idioms.

I. THERE are some phrases which are obvious to the most ordinary apprehensions, as " to honour with honours," " to love with love &c." but it cannot be denied, that they are harsh and unpleasing: of which indeed we need no other proof, than that no person will venture to write or to speak after this manner. Let us contrast this mode of expression in our Vulgar Translation, with what we find in other Versions. Our Blessed Lord describing the state of the Gospel, says, Mark IV. 30. " *With what comparison shall we compare it?*" It is rendered in the Vulgate " aut cui parabolæ comparabimus illud?" which is preferable

ferable to the interpretation by Beza: " Aut quâ collatione contulerimus illud?" and likewise to that by Castalio: " Aut quâ id comparatione comparabimus?" It is in the Version of Mons: " Et par quelle parabole le rapprésenterons-nous?" in the Italian Version: " O, con qual similitudine lo rappresenteremo?" and in the Spanish: " O conque parabolo lo comparemo?" I believe, it will be acknowledged by every unprejudiced reader, that it is better translated in the Vulgate, and in those three Versions, than in our own; for it conveys precisely the same meaning, without offending the ear in the least degree. — Let us consider another instance in this kind. Just before the institution of the Eucharist, Jesus says unto his disciples Luke XXII. 15. "*With desire I have desired* to eat this passover with you before I suffer." It is expressed in the Version of Mons: " J'ai souhaité avec ardeur," in the Italian Version: " Jo ho grandemente desiderato," and in the Spanish: " En gran manera he desseado." Are not the words of the Original επιθυμια επεθυμησα clearly and properly set forth in these Versions: But they cannot be rendered better than in the Geneva, and in the Bishops-Bible: " *I have earnestly desired.*" Why our Translators did not adopt this interpretation, it seems hard to conceive; unless it were for the sake of taking an opportunity to give a marginal reading: " *I have heartily desired,*" which is one of the most frivolous and unnecessary notes that ever appeared in print; for it was impossible for the most unlettered man to mistake their meaning; and neither the text, nor the margin exhibits so good a reading, as what occurs in the Bibles above mentioned. This repetition of the same object, expressed by the Verb and by the Substantive, is the Greek manner of rendering that peculiar form of the Oriental Verbs, called the Conjugation Pihel, by

which

which the intensity of any action is denoted; but in the English language, instead of repeating the object, some Adverb had better be annexed to the Verb, in order to mark the earnestness and frequency of the action. Those who were employed by king James in translating the Old Testament, did not think themselves obliged to adhere strictly to the letter, in rendering phrases in this kind. It is related in Jonah I. 10. " Then were the men *exceedingly afraid*, and said unto him, Why hast thou done this?" It is in the Hebrew: " feared with great fear." Thus also ver. 16. " And the men *feared* Jehovah *greatly*," in the Hebrew: " feared with great fear." Again, IV. 1. " But it *displeased* Jonah *exceedingly*," in the Hebrew: " displeased with great displeasure." So ver. 6. " And Jonah *rejoyced exceedingly* because of the plant," in the Hebrew: " rejoyced with great joy." Thus in the course of four chapters are four exceptions to the rule of a close verbal rendering; a circumstance, which makes it probable, that those who translated the New Testament, did not act sufficiently in concert with those who translated the Old; which undoubtedly ought to have been done, because Hebraisms are so frequent in the New Testament. But this will not appear strange, when we consider, that the translators of the New Testament not only often differ from one another, but sometimes from themselves, in the same chapter, and in the same verse.

II. There is another mode of expression, which frequently occurs; and which cannot but hurt the ear of an English reader: I mean, " answered and said." Sometimes it is used, when we are almost absolutely certain, that no question has been asked. Thus Matth. XI. 25. When Jesus returned thanks unto God for revealing the dispensations of his mercy to the meek, and to the
humble,

humble, our Translators have rendered it "At that time Jesus *answered and said* &c." It is in Castalio: "aliquando Jesus locutus in hunc modum est," in the Version of Mons: "Alors Jesus dit ces paroles," in the Italian Version: "In qual tempo Jesù prese à dire," and in Schmidius: "Illo tempore proloquens Jesus dixit." The Vulgate has *respondens* in this, and in all similar passages; and though Beza observes upon this verse in St. Matthew, that no question was put, and that the Participle αποκριθεις does not at all imply it, yet he preposterously uses the word *respondens*. It is rendered by Dr. Priestley "At that time Jesus took occasion to say," which gives us the genuine sense of the Original, without transferring its disgusting idiom [*]. Sometimes our Translators adopt the phrase above-mentioned, when it is *positively* affirmed, that no question was put. Thus it is said Luke XIV. 3. "that Jesus asked the lawyers and Pharisees, whether it were lawful to heal on the sabbath-day; but they *held their peace* [were silent,] and, after healing the man, Jesus *answered* them, saying, Which of you shall have an ass or an ox fallen into a pit, and will not *straightway* [immediately] pull him out on the sabbath-day?" In this point most Versions are better than ours. It is in that of Mons: "il leur dit ensuite," in the Italian: "Poi fece lor motto e disse," in Castalio: "illosque sic effatus est," and in Tremellius: "et dixit eis." Schmidius renders it absurdly by *respondens*, though in a note he explains it "tunc sermonem orsus dixit," and Beza has *respondens* as above.—There is still a more extraordinary instance in Mark XI. 13. where Jesus is said to return an answer, even to an inanimate thing. "And seeing a fig-tree afar off, having leaves, *he came if haply he might find* [he went if he might happen

---

[*] English Harmony, § xxxiv. p. 90.

pen to find] any thing thereon: (and when he came to it, he found nothing but leaves) *for the time of figs was not yet* [for the season of figs was not come,] *and Jesus answered and said unto it.* It should be " upon which Jesus said unto it." Thus Tremellius " et dixit ficui," and Castalio ," itaque eam sic allocutus est Jesus," and Schmidius upon this occasion expresses himself more properly " tunc orsus sermonem Jesus dixit ficui." The Spanish Version follows the Vulgate; but the French and Italian translations are in this respect perfectly right. Here again Beza exposes himself to censure; for he renders it by *respondens dixit*, notwithstanding he says, that αποκριθεις is a Hebrew pleonasm; and that an answer cannot be made to a tree. Bishop Pearce observes upon Matth. XI. 25. as, in fact, do almost all the commentators, " that by answering, when joined to saying, nothing more is meant than speaking; and that instances of αποκρινεσθαι in this sense are in various passages of the Old and New Testament." It is certain, that none of our early English translators attended to this distinction; nor is it probable, that they ever considered, that the purest writers of antiquity sometimes use the Verb αποκρινεσθαι, not only for " to begin," or " to continue a discourse," but likewise for " to ask a question."

III. The Verb αρχομαι, in the middle Voice, is invariably rendered " to begin," without being looked upon as a Pleonasm. Mr. Markland suspects that αρξαμενος in Luke XXIV. 27. is little more than an expletive, as in many other passages in Scripture *; but we may safely affirm, that it is often quite redundant; and it

---

* See Bowyer's Conjectures on the N. T. p. 193. and Wakefield's note upon Matth. XI. 20. It is a little surprizing, that Parkhurst has not observed in his Lexicon, that Αρχομαι is often used by the writers of the N. T. as a mere expletive.

it will not be amiss to mention first one or two examples, where it is properly rendered. Thus Matth. IV. 17. "From that time Jesus *began* to preach." This is well translated, because it is likely, that our Saviour's ministry commenced from that period. So XVI. 21. "From that time Jesus began *to shew his disciples how that* [to inform his disciples that] he must go unto Jerusalem, and suffer many things *of* [from] the elders &c." Here again it is rightly interpreted, because Jesus then first acquainted his disciples with what was to befall him. On the contrary, there are numberless passages in which this word ought to have been omitted. Thus Matth. XI. 7. "*And as they departed, Jesus began to say unto the multitudes* &c." It should be "And when they were departed, Jesus said unto the multitude &c." It is in the Version of Mons: "Jesus s'adressant au peuple." So XII. 1. "At that time Jesus went on the sabbath-day through the corn, and his disciples were *an hungred, and began to pluck* [hungry, and plucked] the ears of corn &c." — Mark V. 17. " And they *began to pray him* [desired him] to depart out of their *coasts* [borders."] — VI. 7. " And he *calleth* [called] unto him the twelve, *and began to send them forth* [and sent them forth] by two and two &c." — VI. 34. " *And Jesus when he came out saw much people* [And after Jesus was come out of the boat, he saw a great multitude of people] and was moved with compassion towards them, because they were as sheep not having a shepherd, *and he began to teach them* [and he taught them] many things." — XI. 15. " And they *come* [came] to Jerusalem; and Jesus went into the temple, *and began to cast them out that* [and turned them out who] sold and bought in the temple." — Luke III. 8. " Bring forth therefore fruits worthy of repentance; *and begin not to say* [and say not] within yourselves,

we

we have Abraham to our father &c." It is in the Version of Mons: " n'allez pas dire." — XIII. 25. " When once the master of the house is risen up, and hath shut the door, *and ye begin to stand without* &c. [and ye stand without &c."] (26) *Then shall ye begin to say* [Then shall ye say] we have eaten &c." In all these instances, the Verb αρχομαι is evidently an expletive. We find it often used by the LXX. Thus Gen. II. 3. " ότι εν αυτη κατεπαυσεν απο παντων των εργων αυτ8, ὡν ηρξατο ὁ Θεος ποιησαι," that is, " which God had made." So Hof. V. 11. " ότι ηρξατο πορευεσθαι οπισω των ματαιων," that is, " walked after vanities." And we are told by Dr. Lightfoot, that it is a Hebrew pleonasm, which occurs frequently in the Talmud.

IV. There is another expletive, not much unlike the former: I mean, the Verb δοκεω. Thus Matth. III. 9. " *And think not to say within yourselves*, we have Abraham *to* our father." It should be " and say not within yourselves, that we have Abraham *for* our father;" for, as Dr. Lightfoot observes, μη δοξητε λεγειν was a Jerusalem phrase, or pleonasm, much used by the writers of the Talmud. There can be no reason therefore to render it with Schmidius " ne præsumatis dicere," which is uncommonly harsh. Thus again Mark X. 42. " Ye know that *they which are accounted to rule over the Gentiles* &c." It ought to be, " they who rule over the Gentiles," or, " the rulers of the Gentiles ;" for, as Dr. Owen remarks upon this verse, ὁι δοκ8ντες αρχειν is an expletive, signifying nothing more than αρχ8σιν; and I cannot see any ground in what Mr. Parkhurst has advanced to the contrary*. I omit mentioning many similar passages in the New Testament, produced by Dr. Owen, and by other writers. — Under this head we may speak

* See the Verb δοκεω in his Lexicon, — and see also Blackwall's Sacred Classics, p. 59.

speak of the Verb προστίθημι. Thus Luke XIX. 11. "*And as they heard these things, he added, and spake a parable.*" It should be "And while they attended to these things, he spake a parable." The Participle προστιθεις, though rendered in the Vulgate *adjiciens*, and by Beza *pergens*, is redundant; as likewise is προσεθετο in Luke XX. 11. "*And again he sent* [And he sent] another servant." (12) "*And again he sent the third* [And he sent *a* third.]" Few expressions are more commonly used by the LXX, of which I will give two instances from the prophet Amos. V. 2. " επεσεν, ουκετι μη προσθη τε αναςησαι," in the Hebrew: " she shall not add to rise," and in the Vulgar Translation: " she shall no more rise." So VIII. 2. " ουκετι μη προσθω τε παρελθειν αυτον," in the Hebrew: "I will not add to pass," and in the Vulgar Translation: " I will not again pass by them any more." But it would have been better to omit "*again*," which seems to be unnecessary; and which accordingly Bishop Newcome has omitted in his new Version:

I will not pass *through* them any more.

V. What has been hitherto said, relates to modes of expression, intelligible to every class of readers, though always uncouth, and sometimes improperly applied; but there is one phrase, which it is impossible for the common people to understand: " *and he opened his mouth, and said.*" Wetstein tells us that " Ore aperto loqui est clara voce et cum fiducia loqui, et opponitur ei qui clam mussitat et susurrat." Bengelius says, that it always points out a man, who is going to speak with deliberation; and indeed we are informed by most of the commentators, that ανοιξας το ςομα was a phrase used by the Jews, to introduce a subject of importance. These arguments would certainly carry great weight with them,

if

if we did not find the same words used upon ordinary occasions. Thus Luke I. 64. "And his mouth was opened immediately, and he spake." Now how is it possible for the lower ranks of people to know, that in this case the phrase is to be taken according to its general acceptation, and that in others it is to be looked upon as a pure Hebraism, which ushers in a solemn speech? Yet almost all the translators, except Castalio, have rendered both the one and the other by "aperto ore," or, "aperiens os," or by something of the like import; but he has ventured to depart from the letter, and has rendered Matth. V. 2. "Et ille hujusmodi oratione docere aggressus est." Should not this be deemed literal enough, we might translate it here, and in similar passages, *"and he raised his voice and said."*

VI. The last phrase, which I shall speak of, I know not under what class to range; but it is manifest, that nothing can be more harsh or disagreeable: that is, *to sit at meat."* Our Translators seem to have judged well in rendering ανακειμενοι and κατακλινομενοι "sitting:" for it would have been useless, and perhaps impossible, to describe clearly the manner in which the Jews rested on couches at their meals; but why they should not always render it "sitting at table" (as they have done in John XII. 2.) it is hard to determine. The Latin translators have for the most part interpreted it literally by "recumbentes, accumbentes, discumbentes;" but "to be at table," or, "to sit at table," is uniformly found in the Geneva Bible, and in the French, Spanish, and Italian Versions. The expression "to sit at meat" is not only very uncouth, but seems to have been improperly applied upon some occasions. Thus Mark XVI. 14. "Afterward he appeared to the eleven, *as they sat at meat."* Now it is far from being evident, that the disciples were then at their meal; on the contrary, it is more probable, that they were indulging their grief; therefore Beza renders ανακειμενοις αυτοις " una sedentibus ipsis," conformable to which is the Geneva Bible " as they sat together," and there is a marginal reading in it " mourning and praying."—There is likewise a passage in Luke XXIV. 30. where this phrase should not have been admitted. " And it came to pass, as he sat at *meat* with them, he took *bread*." This strange confusion would have been avoided by saying " While he sat at *table* with them, he took bread."—I shall conclude with mentioning two passages of a similar nature, which betray a great want of attention in our Translators. It is said Matth XV. 36. " And he took the seven loaves and the fishes, and gave thanks, *and brake them* [and brake the loaves] and gave *to his disciples* [them to his disciples] and the disciples to the multitude: (37) And they did all eat, and were filled, and they took up of the broken *meat* that was left, seven baskets full." The parallel passage in Mark VIII. 8. is expressed in the same manner. To speak of *meat* remaining from bread and fish, must necessarily disgust an English ear. It ought to be " And they took up seven baskets full of the fragments which were left." It is probable, that, at the time our last Version was made, the word *meat* denoted food in general; and was not confined to the limited sense, in which it is understood at present; but as it then also signified *flesh to be eaten*, it was surely blameable in our Translators to use upon this occasion a term of so ambiguous a meaning.

CHAPTER

CHAPTER XIII.

A Comparison of two Chapters in Cranmer's, and in the Geneva, and in the Bishops Bible, with the same Chapters in our Present Version.

IN the course of these remarks, I have paid a particular attention to our antient English Versions; for it was ordered by James I. "that the Bishops-Bible should be followed by our Translators, and as little altered as the Original would permit; and that the translations of Tyndal, Mathew, Coverdale, Whitchurch, and Geneva should be used, when they come closer to the Original, than the Bishops-Bible." It may not perhaps be unpleasing to the reader, at least it will save him some trouble, if I here give him a specimen of four different Versions; of the respective merit or demerit of which he may the more readily form a judgement, when he can peruse all of them in one view. I shall take one chapter from the Evangelists, and another from the Acts; and I am led to select these from no other motive, than that of their being moderate in their length.

Cranmer's

Cranmer's, or the Great Bible, printed at London, by E. Whitchurch, 1541.	Geneva Bible, the first Edition, printed at Geneva, by Rowland Hall, 1560.

St. MATTHEW,

Whē Jesus was borne at Bethleē a cytie of Jewry, in the tyme of Herode the kynge: Beholde, there came wyse men frō the east to Jerusalem, sayeng: Where is he that is borne kynge of Jewes? For we have sene hys starre in the east, & are come to worshyppe hym.

When Herode the kynge had herde these thynges, he was troubled, and all ỹ cytie of Jerusalem with hym. And whan he had gathered all the chefe prestes and scribes of the people togeather, he demaunded of them, where Christ shulde be borne, And they said unto hym: At Bethleem in Jewrye. For thus it is wrytten by the Prophete: And thou Bethleem in the lande of Juda, art not the leest amonge the princes of Juda. For out of the shal there come unto me the captayne, that shall governe my people Israel.

Then Herode (whē he had prevely called the wyse men) he enquyred of the diligently what time the starre appered, & he bad them go to Bethleem, & said: Go youre way thyther, & search diligētly for ỹ chyld. And whē ye have foūde him, bringe me worde agayne that I may come and worshyp hym also.

When they had herd ỹ kynge, they departed: and lo, the starre whych they saw in the east, went before thē, tyl it came, & stode over the place, wherin the chyld was. Whē they sawe the starre, they were exceedynge glad: and went into the house, and foūde the chyld wyth Mary hys mother, & fel down flat and worshypped hym, and opened their treasures & offered unto hym gyftes, golde, frankinsense, & myrre. And after they were warned of God in slepe (that they shuld not go agayne to Herode) they returned into theyr owne countre another waye.

1. When Jesus then was borne at Bethlehem in Judea, in the dayes of Herode the king, beholde, there came wise-men from the East to Jerusalem,

2. Saying, where is the king of the Jewes that is borne? for we have sene his starre in the East, & are come to worship him.

3. When king Herode heard *this*, he was troubled, and all Jerusalem with him.

4. And gathering together all the chief Priests and Scribes of the people, he asked of them, where Christ shulde be borne.

5. And they said unto him, at Bethlehem in Judea; for so it is written by the Prophet,

6. And thou Beth-lehem in the land of Juda, art not the least among the princes of Juda; for out of thee shall come the governour that shal fede my people Israel.

7. Then Herode prively called the Wisemen, *and* diligently inquired of them the time of the starre that appeared,

8. And sent them to Beth-lehem, saying, Go, and searche diligently for the babe; and when ye have founde him, bring me worde againe, that I may come also, and worship him.

9. So when they had heard the king, they departed: and lo, the starre which they had sene in the East, went before them, til it came, and stode over *the place* where the babe was.

10. And when they sawe the starre, they rejoyced with an exceeding great joye,

11. And went into the house, and founde the babe with Marie his mother, and fel downe, and worshipped him, and opened their treasures, and presented unto him giftes, *even* golde, and incense, and myrrhe.

12. And after they were warned of God in a dreame, that they shulde not go againe to Herode, they returned into their countrey another way.

Parker's, or the Bishop's-Bible, the first Edition, printed at London, by Richard Jugge, 1568.	King James's, or the Present Version, the first Edition, printed at London, by Barker, 1611.
CHAP. II.	
1. When Jesus was borne in Bethlehem, a citie of Jurie, in the dayes of Herode the kyng, beholde, there came wise men from the East to Hierusalem.	1. Now when Jesus was borne in Bethlehem of Judea, in the dayes of Herod the king, behold, there came Wise men from the East to Hierusalem.
2. Saying, Where is he that is borne kyng of Jewes? for we have seene his starre in the East, and are come to worship hym.	2. Saying, where is he that is borne king of the Jewes? for we have seene his starre in the East, and are come to worship him.
3. When Herode the kyng had hearde these thynges, he was troubled, and all [the citie of] Hierusalem with hym.	3. When Herod the king had heard *these things*, he was troubled, and all Hierusalem with him.
4. And when hee hadde gathered all the chiefe Priestes and Scribes of the people together, he demanded of them where Christ shoulde be borne.	4. And when he had gathered all the chiefe Priests and Scribes of the people together, he demanded of them, where Christ should be borne.
5. And they saide unto him, At Bethlehem in Jurie, for thus it is written by the Prophete,	5. And they said unto him, In Bethlehem of Judea; for thus it is written by the Prophet,
6. And thou Bethlehem [in] the lande of Juda, art not the least among the princes of Juda. For out of thee shall there come a capitaine, that shal governe my people Israel.	6. And thou Bethlehem *in* the land of Juda, art not the least among the princes of Juda; for out of thee shall come a Governour, that shall rule my people Israel.
7. Then Herode, when he had privilye called the wyse men, inquired of them diligently, what time the starre appeared.	7. Then Herod, when he had privily called the wise men, enquired of them diligently what time the starre appeared.
8. And he sent them to Bethlehem, and sayde: Go and search diligently for the young childe, and when ye have founde hym, bryng me worde againe, that I may come and worship hym also.	8. And he sent them to Bethlehem, and said, Goe & search diligently for the yong child, and when ye have founde *him*, bring me word againe, that I may come and worship him also.
9. When they had hearde the kyng, they departed, and loe, the starre which they sawe in the East, went before them, tyl it came and stoode over (the place) wherein the young chylde was.	9. When they had heard the king, they departed, and loe, the starre which they saw in the East, went before them, till it came and stood over where the young child was.
10. And when they sawe the starre, they rejoyced exceedingly with great joy.	10. When they saw the starre, they rejoyced with exceeding great joy.
11. And went into the house, and founde the young chylde with Marie his mother, & fell downe, and worshypped hym, and opened their treasures, and presented unto hym gyftes, golde, and frankensence and mirre.	11. And when they were come into the house, they saw the young child with Mary his mother, & fell down & worshipped him; & when they had opened their treasures, they presented unto him, gifts, gold, and frankincense, and myrrhe.
12. And after they were warned of God in a dreame, that they shoulde not go againe to Herode, they returned unto their owne countrey another way.	12. And being warned of God in a dreame, that they should not returne to Herode, they departed into their own countrey another way.

Great Bible.

Whē they were departed, behold, the Angell of the Lorde appered to Joseph in slepe sayenge, aryse, & take the chyld & his mother and flye into Egypt: and be thou there tyl I brynge the worde. For it wyl come to passe that Herode shall seke the chylde, to destroy hym. So when he awoke, he toke the chylde and his mother by nyght, and departed into Egypt, and was there unto the death of Herode, that it myght be fulfylled, whych was spoken of the Lorde by y prophete, sayinge: out of Egypt have I called my sonne.

Then Herode whē he sawe y he was mocked of y wyse mē, he was exceeding wroth, & sent forth mē of warre, & slue al the childrē that were in Bethleem, and in al y coastes (as many as were two yeare olde or under) accordynge to the tyme, whych he had dilygently knowē out of the wyse men.
Then was fulfylled that, whych was spokē by y prophet Jeremye, where as he sayde: in Rama was there a voyce herde lamentacion, wepynge, & great mournynge. Rachel wepynge for her chyldren, & wolde not be coforted because they were not. But when Herode was deade beholde, an angell of the Lorde appeared in a slepe to Joseph in Egypt, sayenge: aryse, and take the chylde of hys mother, and go into the lande of Israel, for they are deade which sought the chyldes lyfe. And he arose, and toke the chylde and hys mother, & came into the lāde of Israel. But when he herde that Archelaus dyd raygne in Jewrye, in the rowme of hys father Herode, he was afrayd to go thither. Notwithstandynge after he was warned of God in a slepe, he turned asyde into y parties of Galilee, and went and dwelt in a cyte which is called Nazareth: that it might be fulfylled whyche was spoken by the prophetes: he shal be called a Nazarite.

Geneva Bible.

13. After their departure, beholde the Angel of the Lord appeareth to Joseph in a dreame, saying, arise and take the babe and his mother, and flee into Egypt, and be there til I bring thee worde; for Herode will seke the babe, to destroye him.

14. So he arose and toke the babe and his mother by night, and departed into Egypt,
15. And was there unto the death of Herode, that it might be fulfilled, which was spoken of the Lord by the Prophet, saying, Out of Egypt have I called my sonne.
16. Then Herode, seing that he was mocked of the wise-men, was exceeding wroth, and sent forthe, and slew all the male children that were in Bethlehem, and in all the coastes thereof, from two yere olde and under, according to the time which he had diligently searched out of the wise-men.
17. Then was that fulfilled which was spoken by the Prophet Jeremias, saying,
18. In Rama was a voyce heard, mourning, and weping, and great lamentation: Rachel weping for her children, and wolde not be comforted, because they were not.
19. And when Herode was dead, beholde, an Angel of the Lord appeareth in a dreame to Joseph in Egypt,
20. Saying, Arise and take the babe and his mother, and go into the land of Israel, for they are dead which soght the babe's life.
21. Then he arose up, and toke the babe and his mother, and came into the land of Israel.
22. But when he heard that Archelaus did reigne in Judea, in steede of his father Herode, he was afrayed to go thether: yet after he was warned of God in a dreame, he turned aside into the parties of Galilee.
23. And went and dwelt in a citie called Nazaret, that it might be fulfilled which was spoken by the prophetes, *which was*, that he shulde be called a Nazarite.

Bishops-Bible.	Present Version.

13. When they were departed, beholde, the Angel of the Lord appeared to Joseph in a dreame, saying, Arise, and take the young chylde and his mother, and flee into Egipte, and be thou there, tyll I bryng thee worde. For it will come to pass, that Herode shall seke the young chyld to destroy hym.

14. When he arose, he toke the young chyld & hys mother by nyght, & departed into Egipt.

15. And was there unto the death of Herode, that it might be fulfylled which was spoken of the Lorde by the Prophete, saying, Out of Egipte have I called my Sonne.

16. Then Herode, when he sawe that he was mocked of the wyse men, was exceeding wroth, and sent foorth, and slew all the chyldren that were in Bethlehem, and in all the coastes as many as were two yere olde or under, according to the tyme, which he had diligently searched out of the wyse men.

17. Then was fulfylled that, which was spoken by Jeremie the prophete, saying,

18. In Rama was there a voyce hearde, lamentation, wepying, and great mournyng, Rachel weping (for her children) and woulde not be comforted, because they were not.

19. But when Herode was dead, beholde, an Angel of the Lorde appeared to Joseph in a dreame in Egypt, saying,

20. Aryse, & take the young chylde & his mother, and go into the lande of Israel, for they are deade, whiche sought the young chylde's life.

21. And he arose, and toke the young chyld and his mother, & came into the lande of Israel.

22. But when he hearde, that Archelaus dyd reigne in Jurie, in the rowme of his father Herode, he was afrayde to go thyther. Notwithstanding, after he was warned of God in a dreame, he turned aside into the parties of Galilee.

23. And (went and) dwelt in a citie, which is called Nazareth, that it myght be fulfylled, which was spoken by the prophetes: He shal be called a Nazarite.

---

13. And when they were departed, behold, the Angel of the Lord appeareth to Joseph in a dreame, saying, Arise, and take the young childe, & his mother, & flee into Egypt, & be thou there until I bring thee word, for Herode will seeke the young childe to destroy him.

14. When he arose, he tooke the young childe & his mother by night, & departed into Egypt.

15. And was there untill the death of Herode, that it might be fulfilled, which was spoken of the Lord by the Prophet, saying, Out of Egypt have I called my Sonne.

16. Then Herode, when hee saw that hee was mocked of the wise men, was exceeding wroth, and sent foorth, & slewe all the children that were in Bethlehem, & in all the coasts thereof, from two yeeres old & under, according to the time which he had diligently enquired of the Wise men.

17. Then was fulfilled that which was spoken by Jeremie the Prophet, saying,

18. In Rama was there a voice heard, lamentation, & weeping, & great mourning: Rachel weeping for her children, & would not be comforted, because they are not.

19. But when Herode was dead, behold, an Angel of the Lord appeareth in a dreame to Joseph in Egypt,

20. Saying, Arise & take the yong childe & his mother, & goe into the land of Israel; for they are dead, which sought the yong childe's life.

21. And he arose, and tooke the yong childe, & his mother, and came into the land of Israel.

22. But when he heard that Archelaus did reigne in Judea, in the roome of his father Herod, hee was afraid to goe thither: notwithstanding, being warned of God in a dreame, he turned aside into the parts of Galilee.

23. And hee came & dwelt in a city called Nazareth, that it might be fulfilled which was spoken by the Prophets, He shall be called a Nazarene.

X   ST.

St. Matthew, Chapter II.

2. Πȣ ἐϛιν ὁ τεχθεις βασιλευς των Ιȣδαιων;] Our Prefent Verfion is conformable to the Vulgate: " Ubi eft ille qui natus eft rex Judæorum?" but it had better have been conformable to the Geneva Bible, or to Coverdale's tranflation: " Where is the *new* borne Kinge of the Jewes?" Thus alfo the Verfion of Mons: " Où eft le Roy des Juifs qui eft *nouvellement* né?" and after the fame manner Mr. Wakefield: " Where is the king of the Jews who is *lately* born?" Beza has rendered it, as in the Zurich Verfion: " Ubi eft ille rex Judæorum qui natus eft?" and he very juftly makes the following obfervation: " Ego vocabulorum collocationem mutavi, ut fenfus effet dilucidior; nam alioqui viderentur magi aliud quærere, nempe, ubi fit ille qui non natus eft privatus, fed rex Judæorum ab ipfis incunabulis, qui fenfus non convenit."

4. πȣ ὁ Χριϛος γενναται.] This fhould have been rendered " where *the* Chrift was to be born," as it is done by Mr. Wynne and Mr. Wakefield; the laft of whom fhews us, that γενναται for μελλει γενεσθαι is not only a Hebraifm, but frequently occurs in Greek authors.

5. Εν Βηθλεεμ της Ιȣδαιας.] Why king James's tranflators preferred " in Bethlehem of Judæa," to " at Bethlehem in Judea" I do not fee.

6. εκ σȣ γαρ εξελευσεται ἡγȣμενος.] Our Prefent Verfion agrees both with the Original, and with the Verfion of the Seventy, in which the Article is not prefixed to ἡγȣμενος: but Cranmer, and the tranflators of the Geneva Bible probably thought, that " *the* captayne" and " *the* governour" or Definite Article was more empha-

emphatically in the ſtyle of prophecy; and we find the ſame in Tyndal, and in Coverdale; however, Wicklif uſes the Indefinite Article: "for of thee *a* duyk ſchal go out that ſchal governe my puple of Iſrael."

8. I have elſewhere had occaſion to make two obſervations upon this verſe.

9. ὁ ἀςηρ ὁν ειδον ἐν τῃ ἀνατολῃ, προηγεν αυτες, ἑως ελθων ἐςη ἐπανω ἑ ἐν το παιδιον.] Here our Preſent Verſion is evidently altered for the worſe in two inſtances. Firſt, ειδον ſhould have been rendered "had ſeen," as in the Geneva Bible, which I mentioned above. Secondly, ἐπανω ἑ ſhould have been rendered "over the place where," or, "wherein," as in the other three Bibles. The ellipſis is ſupplied by Beza, and by the author of the Zurich Verſion.

10. ἐχαρησαν χαραν μεγαλην σφοδρα.] The Adjective *exceeding* is here very improperly uſed for the Adverb *exceedingly*, in three of the Verſions; a fault, which occurs in all ver. 16. and in many other paſſages. It is certainly better rendered ver. 10. in the Biſhops-Bible, than in our Preſent Verſion; but not better than by Tyndal, and Coverdale: "they were marvayloufly glad."

13. Αγγελος Κυριε.] It ſhould have been tranſlated "*an* angel of the Lord," as in ver. 19. I have already taken notice of the improper uſe of the Definite Article in this chapter.

14. Ὁ δε ἐγερθεις.] This expreſſion does not ſeem to be ſufficiently attended to in any of the Verſions, though perhaps that of Geneva comes neareſt to the true ſenſe, as it ſeems to imply that "he immediately aroſe."

15. Ἱνα πληρωθῃ.] It ought to have been rendered here, and in

ver. 23. and in many other chapters " so that was fulfilled," or, " by which was fulfilled." Every commentator hath observed, that the Ἱνα εκβατικον and αιτιατικον are perpetually confounded by the bulk of translators.

16. ανειλε παντας τυς παιδας.] Doth it not seem extraordinary, that three Versions should omit the word *male*, when the Original expressly points it out? The Vulgate, and Castalio, and Beza, have " pueros," the Spanish Version " los niños," and the Italian " i fanciulli." There could not have been the least occasion for Herod to extend his cruel order to the female children.

Ibid. ὁριοις.] Since the word " coast " has now a more limited signification, being not applicable to an inland country, ὁριοις should be rendered " borders," as it has been remarked by others. Beza has " confinio," which is much more unequivocal than " finibus " in the Vulgate.

18. φωνη εν Ραμα ηκυσθη.] Had king James's translators rendered it thus: " In Rama *there was* a voice heard," it would clearly have been an Explicative Sentence; whereas they have made it an Interrogative one by following Cranmer's, and the Bishops Bible: " In Rama *was there* a voice heard. The Adverb *there* being misplaced, which indeed was unnecessary, and omitted in the Geneva Bible, has caused this confusion.

21. και ηλθεν εις γην Ισραηλ.] It should have been translated " went *towards* the land of Israel," for, as Mr. Wakefield observes from Dr. Scott, Joseph was only going *towards* it, when he was informed of Archelaus's succession; and the Preposition εις is used by the best writers in this sense.

23. και ελθων κατωκησεν εις πολιν &c.] The Bishops-Bible, printed by

by Jugge in 1572, and by Barker in 1578, renders the beginning of this verse thus: " And when he was come thither, he dwelt in a city &c." which seems to be better than in any of the other Versions.

Ibid. Ναζωραιος κληθησεται.] Κληθησεται for εςαι is a frequent Hebraism, and found also in Greek writers; of which some instances are given by Mr. Wakefield, who alone seems to have translated it properly: " He *will be* a Nasorean."

Cranmer's, or, The Great Bible.   Geneva Bible.

ACTS

At the same tyme Herode the kynge stretched forth hys hädes to vexe certen of the cögregaciö. And he kylled James the brother of John ⁊ the sworde. And becaufe he fawe ⁊ it pleafed the Jewes he proceded further, and toke Peter alfo. Then were the dayes of swete breade. And when he had caught hym, he put hym in prefon alfo, & delyvered hym to four quaternions of foudyers to be kepte, entendyng after Eafter to brynge hym forth to the people.

And Peter was kept in prefon. But prayer was made without ceafynge of the cögregzacion, unto God for hym. And when Herode wolde have brought hym out unto the people, the same night flept Peter betwene two foudyers bounde ⁊ two chaynes, & the kepers before the dore kepte the prefon. And beholde, the angel of ⁊ Lorde was there prefent, and a lyght fhyned in the habitacion. And he fmote Peter on the fyde, & ftered him up, fayenge, aryfe up quyckly. And his chaynes fell of from his hädes. And ⁊ angel fayd unto hym: gyrde thy felfe, & bynde on thy fandales. And fo he dyd. And he fayeth unto hym: caft thy garmët about the, and folow me. And he came out & folowed hym, & wyft not ⁊ it was truth whyche was done by the angel, but thought he had fene a vifion. When they were paft the fyrft and the feconde watch, they came ũto the yron gate, that leadeth unto the cytie, whych opened to them by the owne accorde. And they went out, and paffed thorow one ftrete, and forthwyth the angell departed from hym.

And when Peter was come to hymfelfe, he fayd; now I knowe of a fuerty, that the Lorde hath fente hys angell, & hath delyvered me out of the hande of Herode, and from all the waytynge for of the people of ⁊ Jewes. And as he confydred the thynge, he came to ⁊ houfe of Mary ⁊ mother of one John, whofe fyrname was

1. Now about that time, Herode the King ftretched forthe his hands, to vexe certeine of the Church.
2. And he killed James the brother of John with the fworde.
3. And when he fawe that it pleafed the Jewes, he proceded further, to take Peter alfo. (Then were the daies of unleavened bread.)
4. And when he had caught him he put him in prifon, and delivered him to foure quaternions of fouldiers to be kept, intending after the Paffeover to bring him forthe to the people.
5. So Peter was kept in prifon; but earneft prayer was made of the Church unto God for him.
6. And when Herode wolde have broght him out unto the people, the fame night flept Peter betwene two fouldiers, bounde with two chaines, & the kepers before the dore kept the prifon.
7. And beholde, the Angel of the Lord came upon them, & a light fhined in the houfe, and he fmote Peter on the fide, & raifed him up, faying, Arife quickly. And his chaines fel of from his handes.
8. And the Angel faid unto him, Girde thy felf, & binde on thy fandales. And fo he did. Then he faid unto him, Caft thy garment about thee, & followe me.
9. So *Peter* came out & followed him, & knewe not that it was true, which was done by the Angel, but thoght he had fene a vifion.
10. Now when they were paft the firft & the feconde watche, they came unto the yron gate that leadeth unto the citie, which opened to them by it owne accorde, & they went out, and paffed through one ftrete, & by & by the Angel departed from him.
11. And when Peter was come to him felf, he faid, Now I know for a trueth, that the Lord hathe fent his Angel, & hath delivered me out of the hand of Herode, & from all the waiting for of the people of the Jewes.
12. And as he confidered *the thing* he came to the houfe of Marie, the mother

Parker's, or, The Bishops-Bible.	King James's, or, the Present Version.
CHAP. XII.	
1. At the same tyme Herode the king stretched foorth his handes to vexe certayne of the Churche.	1. Now about that time, Herode the king stretched foorth his hands, to vexe certaine of the Church.
2. And he killed James the brother of John with the sworde.	2. And he killed James the brother of John with the sworde.
3. And becauſe he ſawe it pleaſed the Jewes, he proceaded further, and toke Peter alſo. (Then were the dayes of ſweete bread)	3. And becauſe he ſawe it pleaſed the Jewes, hee proceeded further, to take Peter alſo. (Then were the dayes of unleavened bread)
4. And when he had caught him, he put hym in pryſon alſo, & delyvered hym to foure quaternions of ſouldiers to be kept, intendyng after Eaſter to bryng hym foorth to the people.	4. And when hee had apprehended him, he put him in priſon, & delivered him to foure quaternions of ſouldiers to keepe him, intending after Eaſter to bring him forth to the people.
5. And Peter was kept in pryſon; but prayer was made without ceaſing of the Churche unto God for hym.	5. Peter therefore was kept in priſon, but prayer was made without ceaſing of the church unto God for him.
6. And when Herode woulde have brought hym foorth unto the people, the ſame nyght ſlept Peter betwene two ſouldiers, bounde with two chaynes, and the kepers before the doore kept the pryſon.	6. And when Herode would have brought him foorth, the ſame night Peter was ſleeping between two ſouldiers, bound with two chaines, & the keepers before the doore kept the priſon.
7. And beholde, the Angel of the Lorde was there preſent, & a lyght ſhyned in the habitation, & he ſmote Peter on the ſyde, & ſtirred him up, ſaying, Aryſe up quickly. And his chaynes fell of from his handes.	7. And beholde, the Angel of the Lord came upon him, & a light ſhined in the priſon; & hee ſmote Peter on the ſide, & raiſed him up, ſaying, Ariſe up quickly. And his chains fell off from his hands.
8. And the Angel ſayde unto hym: Gyrde thy ſelfe, and bynde on thy ſandales. And ſo he dyd. And he ſayeth unto hym: Caſt thy garment about thee, & folow me.	8. And the Angel ſaid unto him, Girde thyſelf, & binde on thy ſandales: And ſo he did. And he ſayth unto him, Caſt thy garment about thee, & follow me.
9. And he came out and folowed hym, and wyſt not that it was trueth which was done by the Angel, but thought he had ſeene a viſion.	9. And hee went out & followed him, & wiſt not that it was true which was done by the Angel, but thought he ſawe a viſion.
10. When they were paſt the firſt & the ſeconde watche, they came unto the yron gate that leadeth unto the citie, which opened to them by the owne accorde; & they went out & paſſed through one ſtreate, & foorth with the Angel departed from hym.	10. When they were paſt the firſt & the ſecond ward, they came unto the yron gate that leadeth unto the citie, which opened to them of his owne accord; & they went out & paſſed on thorow one ſtreet, & forthwith the Angel departed from him.
11. And when Peter was come to hymſelfe he ſayde; Nowe I knowe of a ſuertie, that the Lorde hath ſent his Angel, & hath delivered me out of the hande of Herode, and from all the waytyng for of the people of the Jewes.	11. And when Peter was come to himſelfe, hee ſaid, Now I know of a ſurety, that the Lord hath ſent his Angel, & hath delivered mee out of the hand of Herode, & from all the expectation of the people of the Jewes.
12. And as he conſidered the thyng, he came to the houſe of Marie the mother of	12. And when he had conſidered the thing, he came to the houſe of Mary the

Great Bible.

Marke, where many were gathered togeather in prayer. As Peter knocked at the entrye dore, a damsell came forthe to do herken, named Rhoda. And when she knewe Peter's voyce she opened not the entrye for gladnes, but ran in, & told how Peter stode before the entry. And they sayd unto her: y art mad: But she affirmed y it was even so. Thē sayd they: it is his angel. But Peter cōtinued knockynge: and when they had opened the dore, & sawe hym, they were astonyed. And whē he had beckened unto them w the hande, that they myght holde theyr peace, he tolde them by what meanes the Lord had brought hym out of the preson. And he sayd: go shew these thynges unto James & to the brethren. And he departed, & went into another place.

Assone as it was daye, ther was no lytell ado amōge the soudyers, what was become of Peter. Whē Herode had sought for him, and founde him not, he examined the kepers and commaūded them to be caryed awaye. And he descēded frō Jewry to Cesarea, & there abode. Herode was displeased w them of Tyre & Sidon. But they came all w one accorde to hym, and made intercessyon unto Blastus the kynges chāberlayne, & desyred peace, because theyr countre was noryshed by y kynges provision. And upon a daye appoynted, Herode arrayed hym in royal apparell, & set hym in hys seate, & made an oracion unto thē. And the people gave a showte, sayenge: it is the voyce of a God, and not of a man. And immediately the Angell of y Lorde smote him, because he gave not God the honoure, and he was eaten of wormes & gave up the goost. And the worde of God grewe and multiplyed. And Barnabas & Paul returned to Jerusalem, when they had fultylled theyr offyce, and toke to them John whose syrname was Marke.

Geneva Bible.

of John, whose surname was Marke, where manie were gathered together, & prayed.

13. And when Peter knocked at the entrie dore, a maide came forthe to hearken, named Rhode.
14. But when she knew Peter's voyce, she opened not the entrie dore for gladnes, but ran in & tolde how Peter stode before the entrie.
15. But they said unto her, Thou art mad. Yet she affirmed it constantly, that it was so. Then said they, it is his Angel.
16. But Peter continued knocking, & when thei had opened it, & sawe him, they were astonied.
17. And he beckened unto them with the hand to holde their peace, & tolde them how the Lord had broght him out of the prison. And he said, Go shewe these things unto James & to the brethren. And he departed, & went into another place.

18. Now assone as it was day there was no small trouble among the souldiers, what was become of Peter.
19. And when Herode had soght for him, & founde him not, he examined the kepers & commanded them to be led to death. And he went downe from Judea to Cesarea, & there abode.
20. Then Herode intended to make warre against them of Tyrus & Sidon, but they came all with one accorde unto him, & persuaded Blastus the King's chamberlaine, & they desired peace, because their countrey was nourished by the King's land.
21. And upon a day appointed Herode arayed him self in royal apparel, & sate on the judgement seat, & made an oration unto them.
22. And the people gave a shoute, saying, The voyce of God, & not of man.
23. But immediatly the Angel of the Lord smote him, because he gave not glorie unto God; so that he was eaten of wormes, & gave up the gost.
24. And the worde of God grewe & multiplied.
25. So Barnabas & Saul returned from Jerusalem, when they had fulfilled their office, & toke with them John, whose surname was Mark.

Bishops-Bible.	Present Version.
John, whose firname was Marke, where many were gathered together in prayer.	mother of John, whose firname was Marke, where many were gathered together praying.
13. As Peter knocked at the entrie doore, a damsell came foorth to hearken, named Rhoda.	13. And as Peter knocked at the doore of the gate, a damosell came to hearken, named Rhoda.
14. And when she knewe Peter's voyce, she opened not the doore for gladnesse, but ran in, and tolde howe Peter stoode before the doore.	14. And when she knew Peter's voice, she opened not the gate for gladnes, but ran in, and told how Peter stood before the gate.
15. And they sayde unto her, Thou art mad. But she affirmed that it was even so. Then sayde they: it is his Angel.	15. And they said unto her, Thou art mad. But she constantly affirmed, that it was even so. Then said they, it is his Angel.
16. But Peter continued knocking, & when they had opened the doore, & sawe hym, they were astonied.	16. But Peter continued knocking, and when they had opened *the doore*, & saw him, they were astonished.
17. And when he had beckened to them with the hande, that they might holde their peace, he tolde them by what meanes the Lord had brought hym out of the pryson. And he sayd: Go shewe these thynges unto James & to the brethren. And he departed, & went into another place.	17. But he beckening to them with the hand, to hold their peace, declared unto them how the Lord had brought him out of the prison: And he said, Goe shew these things to James & to the brethren. And he departed, & went into another place.
18. Nowe assoone as it was day, there was no little adoe among the souldiers, what was become of Peter.	18. Now assoone as it was day, there was no small stirre among the souldiers, what was become of Peter.
19. And when Herode had sought for hym, & founde hym not, he examined the kepers, and commanded them to be caryed away. And he descended from Jurie to Cæsarea, and there abode.	19. And when Herode had sought him, & found him not, he examined the keepers, & commanded that they should be put to death. And he went downe from Judea to Cesarea, and there abode.
20. And Herode was displeased with them of Tyre and Sidon: but they came all with one accorde to hym, & made intercession unto Blastus the kynge's chaumberlayne, & desired peace, because their countrey was norished by the kyng.	20. And Herode was highly displeased with them of Tyre & Sidon, but they came with one accord to him, and having made Blastus the king's chamberlaine their friend, desired peace, because their countrey was nourished by the king's countrey.
21. And upon a day appoynted, Herode arayed hym in royall apparell, & set hym in his seate, & made an oration unto them.	21. And upon a set day, Herod arayed in royall apparell, sate upon his throne, and made an oration unto them.
22. And the people gave a shout (saying) It is the voyce of God, and not of a man.	22. And the people gave a shout, *saying*, It is the voice of a God, and not of a man.
23. And immediately the Angel of the Lord smote hym, because he gave not God the honour, and he was eaten of wormes, and gave up the ghost.	23. And immediately the Angel of the Lord smote him, because hee gave not God the glory, & hee was eaten up of wormes, & gave up the ghost.
24. And the worde of God grewe & multiplied.	24. But the worde of God grewe & multiplied.
25. And Barnabas & Saul returned from Hierusalem, when they had fulfylled their office, & toke with them John, whose furname was Mark.	25. And Barnabas and Saul returned from Hierusalem, when they had fulfilled their ministery, & took with them John, whose syrname was Mark.

ACTS, Chapter XII.

1. εκκλησίας.] It is observable, that this word both in the first and sixth verses is rendered in Cranmer's Bible " congregacion," notwithstanding Tyndal had given great offence by the use of this expression.

4. μετα το Πασχα.] It ought undoubtedly to have been translated " after the Passover," as in the Geneva Bible.

5. προσευχη δε ην εκτενης γινομενη υπο της εκκλησιας &c.] Here again king James's translators appear to have followed the worst copies, though perhaps the full force of εκτενης cannot be expressed by one word. It probably would be better thus " but *fervent* and *daily* prayer was made by the Church &c." In the margin of our Present Version is " instant and earnest prayer," which is far preferable to the reading in the text.

7. Αγγελος Κυριου.] It should have been rendered " *an* Angel of the Lord," and not by the Definite Article, as in the four Versions.—So " raised him up" should in all the Versions have been " awakened him." How can a person be directed " to arise" who before was said " to be raised up?" We have the true sense in Coverdale, though harshly expressed " waked him up."

8. και λεγει αυτω, Περιβαλου το ιματιον σου.] For the sake of avoiding ambiguity, it seems better to put the Substantive instead of the Pronoun: " And *the Angel* saith unto him, Cast thy garment about thee." So L'Enfant and Beausobre: " Prenez votre manteau, dit *l'Ange* encore."

9. και εξελθων ηκολουθει αυτω.] Here the Geneva Bible has properly inserted the regular Antecedent *Peter*, which is not in the other three

three Verſions. It is alſo ſupplied by Beza, and Diodati — "ſaw a viſion" is perhaps better than "had ſeen a viſion," becauſe at that time the Angel had not left Peter — "wiſt" is obſolete, as it has been remarked in another place.

10. Διελθοντες δε την πρωτην φυλακην.] There is no doubt, that "watch" expreſſes φυλακη better than "ward," though perhaps "guard" would have been preferable to either — "his owne accord" is now obſolete, ſince *his* is always appropriated to the Maſculine Pronoun. So "*the* owne accorde" and "*it* owne accorde," as in three of the Verſions, are equally gone into diſuſe. We now uſe the Poſſeſſive "*its*."

11. Νυν οιδα αληθως.] I have mentioned above the impropriety of the rendering "Now I know of a ſurety."

16. ανοιξαντες δε ειδον αυτον.] The ellipſis is better ſupplied here by "the doore" than by "it," as in the Geneva Bible — "ſaw him" ſhould have been "ſeen him," as I before obſerved.

17. Κατασεισας δε αυτοις τη χειρι σιγαν.] Here the four Verſions are wrong. It ſhould be "beckened with *his* hand," and not the Definite Article "*the* hand," as it has been already intimated.

20. Ην δε ὁ Ηρωδης θυμομαχων Τυριοις και Σιδωνιοις.] The Geneva Verſion has certainly the beſt rendering, which king James's tranſlators have thrown into the margin. Blackwell obſerves *, that θυμομαχων is a ſtrong word both in ſound and ſignification "made war in his heart." We find this expreſſed in the Zurich Verſion "Herodes autem *animo bellum agitabat* in Tyrios et Sidonios."

21. τακτη δε ἡμερα.] The rendering "a day appointed," as in three of the Verſions, is much preferable to "a ſet day."

Sacred Claſſics, p. 198.

23. ανθ' ων ουκ εδωκε την δοξαν τω Θεω.] It is rather matter of surprize, that king James's translators did not adopt the rendering in the Geneva Bible " because he gave not glorie unto God."— The latter part of this verse has been noticed above.

25. Βαρναβας δε και Σαυλος υπεςρεψαν εξ Ιερυσαλημ.] It is observable, that Cranmer's Bible (as well as the Bishops-Bibles of 1572 and 1578) reads " returned *to* Jerusalem." To account for this reading, we find in Wetstein, that many MSS. and most of the early printed copies have " εις Ιερυσαλημ." Indeed the context does not seem to determine precisely which of the two is the true reading. In the next chapter Paul and Barnabas, from the route which they take, appear to have set out from Antioch; and yet in the 13th verse, when John leaves them, " he returns *to* Jerusalem," and returning *to* any place naturally implies setting out *from* thence.

Ibid. πληρωσαντες την διακονιαν.] Why was διακονια translated in our Present Version differently from the other three Bibles? Barnabas and Saul were sent upon a particular *office*, namely, to relieve the brethren at Jerusalem; and the same word διακονια is rendered " relief" in ch. XI. 29. King James's translators have put the word " charge" into the margin, and inserted into the text " ministry," which gives an improper idea of the function of Barnabas and Saul. This is the third instance of a true rendering being forced into the margin in this chapter, to the prejudice of the text.

From this view of the different translations, the following conclusions may fairly be drawn.

In the first place, it is manifest, that all these translations are

excep-

exceptionable in point of orthography. In Cranmer's Bible we find *which*, *whych*, and *whyche*,—*fayeng*, *fayange*, and *fayinge*,— and the same word spelled two different ways in a variety of places. In the Bishops-Bible are *Egipte*, *Egipt*, and *Egypt*,—*child*, *childe*, and *chylde*,—and, in the same verse, *weping* and *wepyng*,—*be* and *bee*,—*his* and *hys*. Such inaccuracies admit of no excuse. One might reasonably expect to find the Bishops-Bible more exact in this particular, because Archbishop Parker informs us in his preface, "*that the translation was comme out with somme further diligence in the printing*," notwithstanding which assertion it is notorious, that there are not more orthographical errors in Cranmer's, than in the Bishops-Bible. In regard to our Present Version, we cannot judge of the orthography of it by the printed copies, which are now in common use, as they differ so greatly from the ancient ones; especially from the first edition, in which *be* and *bee* occur more than once in the same verse. We even find in Buck's edition, printed in 1629, numberless words spelled in the same manner, as in the two Bibles above-mentioned; and though in one and the same chapter an uniformity in the mode of spelling may have been observed, yet where some of the same words have occurred in other chapters, we often see them differently spelled. If it be said, that this fault is to be charged to the carelessness of the printer, the same argument may be urged with equal justice in favour of the translators of the other Bibles.

Secondly, it appears, that the printing of words in a different character from the text, was not an invention of king James's translators. This kind of refinement was indeed not unknown to Archbishop Cranmer; but it may be seen more at large in the Geneva Bible; and the words in the Bishops-Bible, which are

printed

printed in smaller characters, and inserted within crotchets, are in effect, as well as those in Cranmer's and our Present Version, so many Italics. The utter insignificancy of the greatest part of them in all these Versions cannot escape the observation of an attentive reader. Take the following as a specimen from the chapter of St. Matthew which I have just considered. The Geneva Bible reads ver. 7. " Then Herode prively called the Wise-men, *and* diligently enquired of them." — The Bishops-Bible reads, ver. 6. " And thou Bethlehem [in] the lande of Juda." It is thus also in our Present Version, which affords us in ver. 18. another supplement of the like stamp: " Rachel weeping *for* her children." Could there be the least occasion to discriminate these three words by Italic characters, when the Original virtually implies them, and could not be rendered into English without them? But in Acts VII. 39. there occurs a still stronger instance of the injudicious use of Italics, because the necessity of using them arose from the preceding ungrammatical language of the translators: " To whom our fathers would not obey, but thrust *him* from them." Had the translators written agreeably to the idiom of the English tongue, they would have rendered this passage " Whom our fathers would not obey, but thrust from them." The modern printers have not only implicitly followed their pattern in this instance, but in the very next verse have gone beyond it; for they have distinguished two words by Italics (which were not so distinguished before) for no other reason, it should seem, than to shew, that they had better have been omitted by all: " For *as for* this Moses."

Since we are now speaking of additional Italics, it will not be improper to mention, that in perusing the various English translations siations of the Bible, which the nature of my undertaking necessarily led me to consult, I could not avoid remarking (what indeed has been observed by others) the amazing increase of words printed in Italics, and the unwarrantable freedom taken with them. In the Acts of the Apostles, for instance, the number of words in Italic characters, is, in all the authorized Bibles of the present century, ten times as great as it was in the first copy of king James's Bible: yet this was intended to be, and, it should seem, ought to have been, the standard of all the rest. Now as all the Italics in the first copy of that Bible were, justly speaking, the comments of the translators upon the text *, so all the additional Italics in the modern Bibles may be called with equal propriety the comments of the *printers* or *editors*; and if this be true, as undoubtedly it is, can a reasonable objection lie against a revision of the whole, since these partial alterations have been from time to time quietly admitted from the hands of persons, not only incompetent, but also unauthorized, to make them?— We may here add, that this is not the only liberty which has been taken with king James's Bible; for we find in many of the modern editions a total alteration of the contents prefixed to each chapter. It is hard to conceive, that any other licence can be allowable, than that of correcting the orthography, where common practice and the example of our best writers have made the correction necessary. The contents of the chapters, as well as the chapters themselves, will be subject to a general revision, if ever it should take place; the expediency of which is, I trust, in every point of view, sufficiently established by the foregoing observations.

Thirdly,

---

* See Pilkington's Remarks, p. 177.—and see also Dr. Geddes's Prospectus, p. 64, and his Letter to the late Bishop of London, p. 33.

Thirdly, it may be remarked, that, as far as we can judge from a comparison of the four Versions, the English language received very little improvement during the course of more than half a century; for in general there occurs in all of them the same phraseology; and the same order and construction of words; and what we see in Cranmer, was chiefly copied from Tyndal and Coverdale. It was indeed natural for our last translators to tread closely in the footsteps of those who had gone before them; not more in compliance with the Royal injunctions, than from a conviction, that most of the best words and idioms had been already employed: a circumstance, which, united to several others, leads me to agree intirely with Bishop Lowth, that it is not a *new*, but an *improved* Version which is wanted.

Fourthly, the reader will observe in the two chapters just offered to his view, as well as in many other passages which have fallen within our inquiry, that where our Present Version has deviated from the old translations, the alteration has been frequently for the worse, rather than for the better.

Lastly, this ought to give a check to the zeal of those persons, who peremptorily maintain, that our Present Version is of all others the purest and the most accurate. It perhaps would be difficult to prove, that it is much superior in these respects to the Geneva Bible, which James I. had the weakness to treat with contempt; but we may safely affirm, it would be impossible to shew, that it excels all the other European translations. Those who scruple not to make such hasty and crude assertions, would do well to peruse the Italian Version of Diodati, which is probably the best model of imitation. Here we never meet with any affected ornaments; any forced or unnatural refinements. The

sense

fenſe of the Original is for the moſt part carefully and faithfully repreſented; and the plain and humble manner of the Goſpel is expreſſed in a clear, conciſe, and correct ſtyle, which never offends the ear by the harſhneſs of its terms; nor degenerates into familiar idiom: whence it is no wonder, that, after being ranked among the fine compoſitions in Italy, it is, in fact, what an eminent Critic and Divine wiſhes the Engliſh Bible to become, a Claſſical book to foreigners*.

CHAPTER XIV.
CONCLUSION.

I HAVE now gone through all the particulars, which it was my deſign to examine; but I cannot difmiſs theſe papers, without adding my earneſt wiſhes, that I may not be miſunderſtood in any of the arguments that have been advanced. God forbid that I ſhould be ſuſpected of propoſing any plan, or of harbouring any thought, which might tend to the detriment of true religion! So far am I from pleading the cauſe of ſcepticiſm, that I look upon the Bible as the charter of our ſalvation; and ſincerely concur with the ſentiments of a great and pious writer, whoſe works have not done more honour to this country, than to human nature itſelf: " I gratefully receive, and rejoyce in the

Z light

---

* See Biſhop Newcome's preface to the minor prophets, p. xxxiii.

light of Revelation, which hath set me at rest in many things, the manner whereof my poor reason can by no means make out to me *." But the more frequently I reflect upon the important truths of Christianity, the more ardently I wish to see our Version revised by proper authority: not according to the caprice of licentious interpreters; but expressing the genuine sense of the Sacred writings: not embellished with the false colouring of rhetoric; but, like the Original itself, simple and unadorned: in fine, correct enough to satisfy the learned and the polite: yet plain enough to convince the lowest orders of mankind.

* Locke, vol. I. p. 573. ed. 1727.

ERRATA.

Page   6. in the note, *for* p. xi. *read* p. xl.
    21. l. 6. *for* by itself, *read* of itself.
    34. in the note, *for* canon xii. p. 376. *read* canon xiii. p. 133.
    35. l. 2. *for* Acts XII. *read* Acts XIII.
    36. l. 11. *for* 1756. *read* 1576.
    45. l. 24. *for* ὅτινε, *read* ὅιτινες.
    57. l. 14. *for* ch. XXIII. *read* ch. XIII.
    62. l. 6. *for* and gathered, *read* and had gathered.
    87. l. 14. *for* the 29th verse, *read* the 24th verse.
    104. l. 3. *for* Luke VI. 4. *read* Luke V. 4.
    125. Supply the note thus: " published 1727."
    133. l. 6. *for* surprized, *read* surprizes.
    Ibid. l. 19. *for* and to hear the words of thee, *read* and to hear words of thee.
    151. in the note, *for* p. 193. *read* p. 133.

www.ingramcontent.com/pod-product-compliance
Lightning Source LLC
Chambersburg PA
CBHW020828190426
43197CB00037B/735